RESEARCH BIBLIOGRAPHIES & CHECKLISTS

36

Emile Zola: a selective analytical bibliography

RESEARCH BIBLIOGRAPHIES & CHECKLISTS

RCB

General editors

A.D. Deyermond, J.R. Little and J.E. Varey

ÉMILE ZOLA

a selective analytical bibliography

BRIAN NELSON

Grant & Cutler Ltd
1982

© Grant & Cutler Ltd
1982
ISBN 0 7293 0126 5

I.S.B.N. 84-499-5910-1

DEPÓSITO LEGAL: V. 2.184 - 1982

Printed in Spain by Artes Gráficas Soler, S.A., Valencia

for

GRANT & CUTLER LTD
11, BUCKINGHAM STREET, LONDON, W.C.2.

CONTENTS

Introduction   7

Abbreviations   9

Section Ba: Bibliographical surveys, critical anthologies and
états présents   11

Section Bb: Books, monographs and periodicals wholly or
substantially devoted to Zola   15

Section Bc-h: Articles (including books which contain sections
on or significant references to Zola)
Bc   General   33
Bd   Fiction   76
*L'Argent 76; L'Assommoir 77; Au Bonheur des Dames 82;
La Bête humaine 82; La Confession de Claude 84; La
Conquête de Plassans 84; La Curée 85; La Débâcle 87;
Le Docteur Pascal 88; La Faute de l'abbé Mouret 89;
Fécondité 91; La Fortune des Rougon 91; Germinal 93;
La Joie de vivre 103; Lourdes 104; Madeleine Férat 105;
Les Mystères de Marseille 105; Nana 106; L'Oeuvre 108;
Une Page d'amour 110; Paris 111; Pot-Bouille 111; Le
Rêve 112; Rome 113; Son Excellence Eugène Rougon 113;
La Terre 113; Thérèse Raquin 115; Travail 117; Le
Ventre de Paris 118; Vérité 119; Short Stories 119.*
Be   Theatre, lyric dramas and theatrical adaptations
of Zola's work   122
Bf   Critical works and the Naturalist aesthetic   125
Bg   Journalism   135
Bh   The Dreyfus Affair   138

Index of names   141

INTRODUCTION

The aim of this bibliography is to provide a useful guide for students and a compact reference tool for specialists. I have tried to take account of all material published before January 1980. The bibliography is restricted to secondary material, and almost entirely to critical studies of Zola's life and work; information concerning primary material is readily accessible elsewhere (see, for example, Hemmings's bibliography in Bb53 and the bibliographies published annually in *Les Cahiers naturalistes* since 1974 [Ba5-10]).

I have attempted to list all of the most significant and valuable work in the field; in addition, I have included some items which, although not always of high quality, reflect the historical evolution of Zola criticism and the full range of critical approaches to his work. In cases of doubt, the tendency has been to err on the side of inclusiveness. I have excluded prefaces and introductions to editions (Garnier-Flammarion, Folio, etc.), as well as details of full critical editions (Pléiade, Cercle du livre précieux, L'Intégrale, Garnier). I have not included unpublished theses or items in such relatively inaccessible languages as Serbo-Croat, Slovak, Greek, Japanese, Russian and Polish. On the other hand, I have judged several reviews (Bc31, 47, 176, 205, 317; Bd43, 215) of secondary works substantial enough to be included: review-articles (Bc315, 356, 359, 377) are also generally included. Only in exceptional cases (e.g., Bc232) have I noted separately articles which have subsequently been incorporated into books. The place of publication of all books in French is Paris unless otherwise marked. In the case of books published by university presses, unless otherwise indicated the place of publication may be assumed to be that of the imprint. Those items (Bc56, 123) which I have been unable to see personally are marked with an asterisk. I should be most grateful for any information or suggestions with regard to errors and omissions. It is fortunate that the policy of this series is to issue supplements in order to keep the bibliographies as complete and up-to-date as possible.

I have annotated those items which I consider to be of particular interest or importance, from either an interpretative or a historical point of view, or whose titles are not self-explanatory. The comments are designed to indicate the scope and viewpoint of items rather than to provide detailed critical evaluation. Whenever an item is closely related or makes specific reference to another item, this is indicated by means of a cross-reference.

Items are numbered serially within each section and are arranged alphabetically by author. The section on Fiction (including short stories) has been further divided alphabetically by novels. The absence of an A prefix in the notation of items is explained by the desire for consistency with the rest of the series (where A has been used to denote primary material).

In preparing this volume I have consulted the standard bibliographies, but my greatest debt is inevitably to David Baguley's invaluable *Bibliographie de la critique sur Emile Zola, 1864-1970* (Ba4), and to the bibliographies published annually since 1974 in *Les Cahiers naturalistes*. I wish to thank the British Academy for a grant which enabled me to carry out work for this book at the Bibliothèque nationale. I am grateful to Roland Desné, Christine Kennedy and John Trethewey, who all helped in different ways. Finally my thanks are due to Professor Roger Little for his constant advice and encouragement.

Aberystwyth, October 1980   Brian Nelson

ABBREVIATIONS

AUMLA	*Journal of the Australasian Modern Language and Literature Association*
CAIEF	*Cahiers de l'Association internationale des études françaises*
CN	*Les Cahiers naturalistes*
CUP	Cambridge University Press
FMLS	*Forum for Modern Language Studies*
FR	*French Review*
FS	*French Studies*
MF	*Mercure de France*
MLN	*Modern Language Notes*
MLQ	*Modern Language Quarterly*
MLR	*Modern Language Review*
NCFS	*Nineteenth-Century French Studies*
NFS	*Nottingham French Studies*
NRF	*Nouvelle Revue française*
OUP	Oxford University Press
PMLA	*Publications of the Modern Language Association of America*
P.U.F.	Presses universitaires de France
RDM	*Revue des deux mondes*
RHLF	*Revue d'histoire littéraire de la France*
RLC	*Revue de littérature comparée*
RR	*Romanic Review*
RSH	*Revue des sciences humaines*
S	*Symposium*
TLLS	*Travaux de linguistique et de littérature* (Strasbourg)
Coll.	Collection

ed.	editor/edited by
Edn(s)	Edition(s)
EZ/Z	Emile Zola/Zola
n.d.	no date given
n.s.	nouvelle série/new series
repr.	reprinted/repris
s.d.	sans date
tr.	translated by

SECTION Ba

Bibliographical surveys,
critical anthologies and *états présents*

Ba1 Anon., 'Z en Russie. Bibliographie établie par la Bibliothèque d'Etat de littératures étrangères. Juin 1960', *CN*, 20 (1962), 180-4.

Ba2 Anon., 'EZ en U.R.S.S. (1960-1963): Bibliographie établie par la Bibliothèque d'Etat de l'U.R.S.S. pour la littérature étrangère', *CN*, 29 (1965), 88-90.

Ba3 Baguley, David, 'Z devant la critique de langue anglaise (1877-1970)', *CN*, 43 (1972), 105-23.

Ba4 ——, *Bibliographie de la critique sur EZ. 1864-1970*, Univ. of Toronto Press, 1976.
An invaluable reference work, chronologically arranged, admirable in its near-exhaustive coverage (nearly 8,000 items are listed) and excellent subject indexes.

Ba5 ——, and B.H. Bakker, 'Bibliographie 1970-1972', *CN*, 47 (1974), 106-19.

Ba6 ——, and B.H. Bakker, 'Bibliographie 1973-1974', *CN*, 49 (1975), 177-90.

Ba7 ——, and B.H. Bakker, 'Bibliographie', *CN*, 50 (1976), 224-35.

Ba8 ——, and B.H. Bakker, 'Bibliographie', *CN*, 51 (1977), 247-53.

Ba9 ——, and B.H. Bakker, 'Bibliographie', *CN*, 52 (1978), 241-53.

Ba10 ——, and B.H. Bakker, 'Bibliographie', *CN*, 53 (1979), 201-12.

Ba11 Balzer, Hans, 'Bibliographie d'EZ en République Démocratique Allemande', in Bb34, pp. 232-3.

Ba12 Becker, Colette, ed., *Les Critiques de notre temps et Z*, Garnier, 1972.

An anthology of criticism published since 1952. Testifies to the vitality
of modern Z criticism and reflects both the diversity of critical approaches
to Z and the richness of his work. The criticism is grouped under five headings: [the man] 'derrière la légende'; Z 'théoricien et critique'; Z 'témoin
de son temps'; 'l'artiste'; 'l'univers imaginaire et symbolique de Z' (easily
the longest section). English and American criticism is inadequately represented. Contains a useful (but often inaccurate) bibliography.

Ba13   Chevrel, Yves, 'Un état présent des études sur Z par un roman-
iste allemand', *CN*, 45 (1973), 101-3.
A synopsis of Ba32.

Ba14   Daus, Ronald, *Z und der französischer Naturalismus*, Stuttgart:
Metzler, 1976.
An analytical thematic bibliography containing about 1,000 items pubd
since the 1870s. Accords particular attention to works on the historical
and intellectual background to Naturalism and studies with a 'philosophico-
sociological' orientation; neglects formal criticism. Contains numerous typo-
graphical errors and some incomplete refs.

Ba15   Dezalay, Auguste, *Lectures de Z*, Armand Colin, 1973.
A reasonably comprehensive analytical survey – with abundant quotations –
of the historical evolution of Z criticism and the wide range of critical
approaches (biographical, genetic, thematic, psychoanalytic, stylistic) to
his work. Concentrates on modern (i.e., post-1952) criticism. Contains a
useful classified bibliography and a filmography.

Ba16   Girard, Marcel, 'Situation d'EZ', *RSH*, 66 (1952), 137-56.
A review of Z's reputation on the fiftieth anniversary of his death. Contains
some perceptive remarks on his personality and on the subjective aspects
of his work.

Ba17   ——, 'EZ et la critique universitaire', *CN*, 1 (1955), 27-33.
Contains some revealing observations on Z's neglect by academic critics.

Ba18   Hemmings, F.W.J., 'The Present Position in Z Studies', *FS*, X
(1956), 97-122; repr. in Charles B. Osburn, ed., *The Present
State of French Studies. A Collection of Research Reviews*,
Metuchen, N.J.: Scarecrow Press, 1971, pp. 586-623.
A penetrating *bilan* of critical work since about 1920, with useful suggest-
ions for future research.

Ba19   ——, 'Z par delà la Manche et l'Atlantique (essai bibliographique)',
CN, 23 (1963), 299-312.
An account of books and articles in English on Z from 1953 to 1962.

Ba20   Le Blond, Maurice, 'EZ dans la presse parisienne de l'entre deux guerres. Index chronologique', *CN*, 29-35 (1965-68), 38 (1969).

Ba21   Lethbridge, Robert, 'Twenty Years of Z Studies (1956-1975)', *FS*, XXXI (1977), 281-93.
A thorough and sensible assessment of the main trends.

Ba22   Menichelli, Gian Carlo, 'EZ e la critica francese', *Nuova Antologia*, CDLXVIII (1956), 513-24.
On trends in Z criticism since 1902.

Ba23   ——, 'L'accueil critique des premières oeuvres de Z (1864-1869). Vers une bibliographie intégrale', *CN*, 53 (1979), 124-31.

Ba24   ——, *Bibliographie de Z en Italie*, Florence: Institut français, 1960.
A painstaking assemblage (with an introduction) of 1094 Italian biblio-graphical refs to Z's work from 1873 to 1958: 7 contributions by Z to Italian periodicals, 17 letters to various individuals, 247 refs to Italian translations of his work, and 823 critical items (books and articles).

Ba25   Olrik, Hilde, 'A propos des *Rougon-Macquart*', *Revue romane* (Copenhagen), I (1966), 88-103.
A review of 'quelques-uns des points culminants de la critique sur Z' (Bb99; Bc379, 387; Bd167) and of perspectives which remain to be explored.

Ba26   Paris, Renzo, ed., *Interpretazioni di Z*, Rome: Savelli, 1975.
An extensive selection of extracts from critics from Z's time to the present day. Contains a useful introduction.

Ba27   Ricatte, Robert, 'A la recherche de Z', *L'Information littéraire*, 2 (March-April 1954), 67-72.

Ba28   Schor, Naomi, 'Z and *la nouvelle critique*', in Bb32, pp. 11-20.

Ba29   Speirs, Dorothy, 'Etat présent des études sur *les Quatre Evan-giles*', *CN*, 48 (1974), 215-35.

Ba30   Suwala, Halina, 'Z en Pologne', *CN*, 20 (1962), 185.

Ba31   Thomson, C.R., 'Index des *Cahiers naturalistes*, années 1955-1974 (numéros 1 à 48)', *CN*, 49 (1975), 191-233.

Ba32   Wolfzettel, Friedrich, 'Zwei Jahrzehnte Z-Forschung', *Romanist-isches Jahrbuch* (Hamburg), XXI (1970), 152-80.

See also Bb81, 97.

SECTION Bb

Books, monographs and periodicals
wholly or substantially devoted to Z

Bb1   Abastado, Claude, *'Germinal': analyse critique* (Profil d'une
       oeuvre, 8), Hatier, 1970.
       A schematic introduction for students.

Bb2   Åhnebrink, Lars, *The Influence of EZ on Frank Norris*,
       Cambridge, Mass.: Harvard U.P., 1947.

Bb3   Alexis, Paul, *EZ,notes d'un ami*, Charpentier, 1882.
       A respectful biography and *apologie* for Z's literary theories. Includes
       some of Z's hitherto unpubd verse.

       ——: see Bb7.

Bb4   Allard, Jacques, *Z. Le Chiffre du texte. Lecture de
       'L'Assommoir'*, Montreal: Les Presses de l'Université du
       Québec; Presses universitaires de Grenoble, 1978.
       A subtle and original analysis of narrative discourse in *L'Assommoir*
       from the point of view of the novel's spatial patterns.

Bb5   Auriant, L., *La Véritable Histoire de 'Nana'*, Mercure de
       France; Brussels: Edns N.R.B., 1942.
       An anecdotal account of the composition of *Nana*, Z's documentation,
       and critical reactions to the novel. Cf. Bd 250-5.

Bb6   Baguley, David, *'Fécondité' d'EZ. Roman à thèse, évangile,
       mythe*, Univ. of Toronto Press, 1973.
       A thorough evaluation of a neglected novel. Part One treats the
       documentary basis (the contemporary concern with the declining
       French birth rate); Part Two describes Z's preparatory work for the
       novel and the critical responses it provoked; Part Three offers a sensible
       interpretation which relates the novel to Z's total output and shows that
       the celebration of procreation and the family is a theme which is
       discernible throughout *Les Rougon-Macquart*.

Bb7 Bakker, B.H., ed., *'Naturalisme pas mort'. Lettres inédites de Paul Alexis à EZ, 1871-1900*, Univ. of Toronto Press, 1971.
A scrupulous, amply documented edition of the 229 letters exchanged between Z and Alexis, his staunchest supporter and first biographer (see Bb3). The letters include extensive personal trivialities but they afford numerous insights into the social, journalistic, literary and theatrical background to Naturalism. Cf. Bc16.

Bb8 Barbusse, Henri, *Z*, Gallimard, 1932; tr. M.B. and F.C. Green, London: Dent, 1932.
A lively general study. Criticizes Z's politics at length, but commends his ultimate advocacy of socialism.

Bb9 Becker, Colette, *'L'Assommoir': analyse critique* (Profil d'une oeuvre, 35), Hatier, 1972.
A schematic introduction for students.

Bb10 Bédé, Jean-Albert, *EZ* (Columbia Essays on Modern Writers, 69), New York: Columbia U.P., 1974.
Limitations of space (48 pp.) impose excessive superficiality on this essay, in which the author attempts to offer a comprehensive account of Z's life and works for English-speaking readers.

Bb11 Bernard, Marc, *Z par lui-même*, Seuil, 1952.
A thin, poorly selected compilation of extracts from Z's fiction; the commentary is banal, though the illustrations (as always in this series) are good.

——, ed.: see Bb90.

Bb12 Bertrand-Jennings, Chantal, *L'Eros et la femme chez Z. De la chute au paradis retrouvé*, Klincksieck, 1977.
A well-argued feminist reading of Z which attributes his preoccupation with destructive femininity and his patriarchal attitudes to the baleful legacy of the Judaeo-Christian tradition. Overlaps on some points with Bb13. Cf. Bb62; Bc207; Bd267, 269.

Bb13 Borie, Jean, *Z et les mythes, ou de la nausée au salut*, Seuil, 1971.
A brilliant psychoanalytic interpretation. Argues that the underlying unity and coherence of Z's work rest on the working-out of Oedipal conflicts: sexuality is the inner spring of Z's work, whose richness lies not in its historical, sociological or documentary value, but in its articulation of a 'difficile nettoyage du corps et du monde'.

Bb14   Brady, Patrick, *'L'Oeuvre' d'EZ. Roman sur les arts, manifeste, autobiographie, roman à clef*, Geneva: Droz, 1967.
A meticulous study − indeed somewhat overwritten − of a problematic, highly autobiographical novel. Examines Z's sources (both personal and literary); his manuscripts and preparatory notes (paying particular attention to the *Ebauche* which is reproduced *in extenso* in an appendix); each character and painting in the novel (including Claude Lantier's relationship to Cézanne, Manet and Impressionism, advancing the argument that through the failure of his artist-protagonist Z is deploring the artistic tendencies of his time, viz. a return to rococo art in particular and decadent, Romantic art in general); structure and narrative techniques. Neglects the central theme of the psychology of artistic creation (especially the erotic/ aesthetic relationship), but clearly demonstrates the importance of *L'Oeuvre* for an understanding of Z's personality and conception of art.

Bb15   Brandes, Georg, *EZ*, Berlin: Eckstein, 1889.
A brief monograph.

Bb16   Brown, Calvin S., *Repetition in Z's Novels*, Athens, Georgia: Univ. of Georgia Press, 1952.
A thorough analysis and classification of the various forms assumed by a salient feature of Z's style. There is little or no comment, however, on the development of Z's use of the device, literary influences and the degree of conscious intention involved. Cf. Bc53, 54, 82, 171, 251.

Bb17   Bruneau, Alfred, *A l'ombre d'un grand coeur. Souvenirs d'une collaboration*, Fasquelle, 1932.
A full account by Z's librettist of his professional collaboration with Z.

Bb18   *Bulletin de la Société littéraire des amis de Z* (1922-38).

Burns, C.A., ed.: see Bb23.

Bb19   *Cahiers de l'Association internationale des études françaises*, XXIV (May 1972), 94-184.
Contains Bc115, 159, 192; Bd21, 195.

Bb20   *Les Cahiers Naturalistes* (1955- -).
Superseded Bb18.

Bb21   Carter, Lawson A., *Z and the Theater*, New Haven: Yale U.P., 1963.
A useful account of Z's dramatic works and librettos, and a well-researched analysis of his dramatic theories, criticism and influence.

Bb22   Case, Frederick Ivor, *La Cité idéale dans 'Travail' d'EZ*, Univ. of Toronto Press, 1974.
A searching but fragmentary analysis of Z's social attitudes as mirrored in *Travail*. Brings out the eclectic nature of the brand of socialism reflected in the novel, the paternalism embodied in Luc Froment, and the simplifications, lacunae and misunderstandings of contemporary socialist thought involved in Z's blueprint for Utopia.

Bb23   Céard, Henry, *Lettres inédites à EZ*, ed. C.A. Burns, Nizet, 1958.
An excellent edition of 241 letters and notes. Constitutes a kind of *journal littéraire* of the period 1877-93 and shows how Céard contributed to the substance of *Une Campagne* (the series of articles Z wrote for *Le Figaro* in 1880-1) and supplied documentation for several of Z's novels (notably *Nana* and *Pot-Bouille*).

Bb24   Cogny, Pierre, *Z et son temps*, Larousse, 1977.
A series of extracts and short commentaries for students.

———, ed.: see Bb84.

Bb25   Conrad, Michael Georg, *EZ*, Berlin: Bard & Marquardt, 1906.
An enthusiastic study by a leading proselytizer of Z in Germany.

Bb26   De Faria, Neide, *Structures et unité dans 'les Rougon-Macquart' (la poétique du cycle)*, Nizet, 1977.
A rigorous application of the techniques of modern structural analysis to *Les Rougon-Macquart*, considered as a single, unified 'text'; focuses on six 'representative' novels: *Germinal*, *L'Assommoir*, *Nana*, *La Bête humaine*, *Le Ventre de Paris* and *L'Oeuvre*.

Deffoux, Léon, ed.: see Bb74.

Bb27   De Lattre, Alain, *Le Réalisme selon Z. Archéologie d'une intelligence*, P.U.F., 1975.
An important reappraisal of the conceptual infrastructure of *Les Rougon-Macquart*. Rather than a conventional study of sources and influences, seeks to correlate and juxtapose *Les Rougon-Macquart* with the scientific theories of Claude Bernard, Darwin and Prosper Lucas; in so doing, contests Z's reputation as a naïve theoretician, poor imitator of Balzac and inveterate pessimist.

Bb28   Descotes, Maurice, *Le Personnage de Napoléon III dans les 'Rougon-Macquart'*, Lettres modernes, 1970.
A straightforward monograph which brings out Z's hostility towards Louis

Napoleon's corrupt, autocratic régime and its various supporters. Might have pointed out more clearly the fact that specifically anti-Imperial satire is restricted almost entirely to the earlier Rougon-Macquart novels, written before the firm establishment of the Third Republic with the centre-left coalition of 1877.

Bb29   Desprez, Louis, *Lettres inédites de Louis Desprez à EZ*, ed. Guy Robert, Les Belles Lettres, 1952.
Cf. Bc109.

Bb30   Doucet, Fernand, *L'Esthétique de Z et son application à la critique*, The Hague: De Nederlandsche Boek- en Steendrukkerij, 1923.
Still worth reading.

Bb31   Dubois, Jacques, *'L'Assommoir' de Z. Société, discours, idéologie* (Col. 'Thèmes et textes'). Larousse, 1973.
Eclectic practical applications of contemporary literary theory (predominantly 'sociocritical') which treat *L'Assommoir* as an autonomous 'text' and attempt to illustrate Barthes's notion of the textual plurality of even the most classical work. Four sections focus on the novel's thematic structure ('Le modèle héroïque', 'Le décor symbolique', 'L'investissement sociologique', 'L'inscription idéologique') and two on techniques ('Prépondérance d'une technique', 'Le soliloque, la rumeur et le roman parlé'). The analysis of Z's use of 'le discours indirect libre' is particularly accomplished. A provocative and illuminating study.

Bb32   *L'Esprit créateur*, XI (Winter 1971).
Contains Ba28; Bc7, 393; Bd28, 134, 290.

Bb33   *Europe*, 83-4 (1952).
Contains Bc108, 127, 339, 341; Bd5, 8, 30, 95, 273, 298, 320, 321; Bf50; Bh15.

Bb34   *Europe*, 468-9 (1968).
Contains Ba11; Bc39, 40, 47, 85, 111, 119, 152, 174, 201, 221, 251, 281, 319, 323, 331, 347, 352; Bd2, 48, 66, 76, 115, 127, 207, 363, 382; Bf10, 19, 24, 31, 66, 71; Bg6; Bh6.

Bb35   Euvrard, Michel, *Z* (Classiques du XXe siècle, 86), Edns universitaires, 1967.
A competent introductory survey.

Bb36   Faguet, Emile, *Z*, Eyméoud, 1903.

A hostile general assessment (31 pp.). Attacks Z for his narrowness of vision, wild romanticism, pornographic excesses and stylistic crudity. Cf. Bc56.

Bb37 Frandon, Ida-Marie, *Autour de 'Germinal'. La Mine et les mineurs*, Geneva: Droz; Lille: Giard, 1955.
A scholarly study of the sources and genesis of the novel.

Bb38 ——, *La Pensée politique d'EZ*, Champion, 1959.
A short monograph (28 pp.). Concentrates almost exclusively on illustrating Z's love for the Republic and his view of the progressive debasement of parliamentarianism with extensive quotations from *Paris* and the parliamentary reports Z wrote for *La Cloche* in 1871-2.

Bb39 Franzén, Nils-Olof, *Z et 'La Joie de vivre'; la genèse du roman, les personnages, les idées*, Stockholm: Almqvist & Wicksell, 1958.
Contains a meticulous analysis of the genesis of the novel as revealed by the manuscript notes, a lucid exploration of the intriguing autobiographical elements in the depiction of the neurotic Lazare Chanteau (which give the novel its distinctive place in the Rougon-Macquart series), and a cogent discussion of the work as a novel of ideas (Lazare's pessimism compared with Pauline's vitalism – an early reflection of Z's later Utopianism). Demonstrates that Z's mind and personality were much more complex than is often assumed.

Bb40 *French Review*, XLIV (Winter 1970-1).
Contains Bd201, 267.

Bb41 Fréville, Jean, *Z, semeur d'orages*, Edns sociales, 1952.
A general study written from a Marxist standpoint. Contains a cogent critique of Z's ideology with particular reference to *L'Assommoir*, *Germinal* and *L'Argent*.

Bb42 Frey, John A., *The Aesthetics of the 'Rougon-Macquart'*, Madrid: José Porrúa Turanzas, 1978.
A valuable study which uses classical stylistic analysis to explore the extent and limits of the aesthetic affinities between Naturalism, Impressionism and Symbolism.

Bb43 Genuzio, Joseph, *Jules Guesde et EZ, ou le socialisme dans l'oeuvre d'EZ*, Bari: Tipografia Levante, 1964.

Bb44 *'Germinal'. Projet sur un roman*, ed. Daniel Lindenberg, Jean-Pierre Vincent, Michel Deutsch and Jacques Blanc, Christian

Bourgois, 1975.
Contains Bc71; Bd185.

Bb45   Girard, Marcel, *'Germinal' de Z* (Coll. 'Poche critique'), Hachette, 1973.
An excellent global study. Cf. Bd167.

Bb46   Grand-Carteret, John, *Z en images. 280 illustrations, portraits, caricatures, documents divers*, Félix Juven, 1908.

Bb47   Grant, Elliott M., *Z's 'Germinal'. A Critical and Historical Study*, Leicester U.P., 1962.
A methodical exposition of the novel's sources and composition, but somewhat marred by the disjunction between the careful examination of Z's documentation and the flatness of the brief chapter on his art, which, given the nature of the study, could have said more about the creative process. An appendix includes a complete transcript of the *Ebauche*.

Bb48   ——, *EZ* (TWAS, 10), New York: Twayne, 1966.
A serviceable general introduction for those unfamiliar with Z. Mainly expository. The treatment of the thematic structure and literary qualities of Z's work is thin in comparison with the discussion of documentation, sources and historicity.

Bb49   Grant, Richard B., *Z's 'Son Excellence Eugène Rougon': An Historical and Critical Study*, Durham, North Carolina: Duke U.P., 1960.
An informative study of Z's only purely political novel. Concentrates on the novel's genesis and composition, and on its historical sources and models, commenting on Z's desire to be both impartial and satirical. Excessive stress on the historicist approach produces an inadequate treatment of the relationship between documentation and the creative process.

Bb50   Guillemin, Henri, *Z, légende et vérité*, Julliard, 1960; Union générale d'édns (série 10/18), 1971.
Mainly concerned with arguing – selectively and unconvincingly – that Z was one of those 'chrétiens qui s'ignorent' (Péguy).

Bb51   ——, *Présentation des 'Rougon-Macquart'*, Gallimard, 1964.
A series of impressionistic, and often eccentric, prefaces to the Rougon-Macquart novels. Strongly biographical in approach. Emphasizes Z's subversion of bourgeois attitudes to sex, money, politics and religion.

Bb52   Gumbrecht, Hans-Ulrich, *Z im historischen Kontext. Für eine*

neue Lektüre des Rougon-Macquart-Zyklus, Munich: Wilhelm Fink, 1978.
An unflinchingly historicist reading.

Bb53 Hemmings, F.W.J., *EZ*, Oxford: Clarendon Press, 1953; 2nd edn 1966.
The principal general study of Z in English. A work of authoritative scholarship and balanced critical judgments. The second edn is substantially different from the first, supplementing the broadly 'sociological' approach of the earlier edn with more stress on the manifestation of unconscious preoccupations in Z's work.

Bb54 ——, *The Life and Times of EZ*, London: Elek, 1977.
Designed as a biographical complement to Bb53. Aimed at non-academic readers, handsomely illustrated and admirably written, this (relatively concise) book is a skilful synthesis of new material. Provides an informative and richly anecdotal account of the external facts of Z's life and a shrewd evocation of his personality. Sets his work very effectively against the background of his age. Frustratingly brief on his psychological make-up and on his intellectual attitudes and their development.

Bb55 Hewitt, Winston R., *Through Those Living Pillars: Man and Nature in the Works of EZ*, The Hague: Mouton, 1974.
A synoptic account of the roles of nature in Z; fails to address itself to the many issues the subject raises.

Bb56* Hofmann, Werner, *'Nana': Mythos und Wirklichkeit*, Cologne: Schauberg, 1973.

Bb57 Huysmans, J.-K., *Lettres inédites à EZ*, ed. Pierre Lambert, Geneva: Droz, 1953.
A copiously annotated edition of 60 letters written during the period 1877-96. Contains a useful introduction by Pierre Cogny entitled 'Perspectives d'une amitié littéraire'.

Bb58 Jagmetti, Antoinette, *'La Bête humaine' d'EZ. Etude de stylistique critique*, Geneva: Droz, 1955.
An exploration of Z's determinism through the novel's imagery and poetic symbolism.

Jennings, Chantal: see Bb12.

Bb59 Kamm, Lewis, *The Object in Z's 'Rougon-Macquart'*, Madrid: José Porrúa Turanzas, 1978.

A systematic study of the ways in which Z's use of the object both translates his vision of life and contributes to the universality of *Les Rougon-Macquart*.

Bb60   Kanes, Martin, *Z's 'La Bête humaine': A Study in Literary Creation*, Berkeley: Univ. of California Press, 1962.
A distinguished study of the genesis of *La Bête humaine*. The analyses of the creative process and the relationship between documentation and imagination are particularly penetrating.

Bb61   King, Graham, *Garden of Z. EZ and his Novels for English Readers*, London: Barrie & Jenkins, 1978.
An enthusiastic but discriminating panorama of Z's life and work aimed at non-academic English readers. Includes an appendix which lists all English translations of Z.

Bb62   Krakowski, Anna, *La Condition de la femme dans l'oeuvre d'EZ*, Nizet, 1974.
A detailed survey and classification of Z's women which has neither the feminist commitment nor the critical sophistication of Bb12. Contains disproportionate emphasis on Z's libertarian, anti-Romantic treatment of women.

Bb63   Kranowski, Nathan, *Paris dans les romans d'EZ*, P.U.F., 1968.
A rather superficial general survey which relies too heavily on paraphrase and summary, and suffers from the lack of a clearly defined approach to the subject. Cf. Bb79.

Lambert, Pierre: see Huysmans, J.-K.

Bb64   Lanoux, Armand, *Bonjour, Monsieur Z*, Amiot-Dumont, 1954; Hachette, 1962; Livre de poche, 1962; revised, Grasset, 1978. English tr. (slightly abridged): *Z*, tr. Mary Glasgow, London: Staples, 1955.
A *biographie romancée* which is detailed and reliable in its factual information and perspicacious in its critical comments.

Bb65   Lapp, John C., *Z before the 'Rougon-Macquart'*, Univ. of Toronto Press, 1964. French tr.: *Les Racines du Naturalisme: Z avant 'Les Rougon-Macquart'*, tr. Danielle Lapp, Bordas, 1972.
Analyses the extent to which certain patterns of plot, character, situation and image which occur constantly in *Les Rougon-Macquart* are prefigured in the early novels and stories. Provides many sensitive insights into the themes and techniques of Z's mature work and makes a valuable contri-

bution to our knowledge of the evolution of his art.

Bb66 Le Blond, Maurice, *Les Projets littéraires d'EZ au moment de sa mort d'après des documents et manuscrits inédits*, Mercure de France, 1927; repr. in *MF*, CXCIX (1927), 5-25.

Bb67 ——, *La Publication de 'La Terre'* (Coll. 'Les Grands Evénements littéraires'), Malfère, 1937.
Very largely superseded by Bb99.

Bb68 Le Blond-Z, Denise, *EZ raconté par sa fille*, Fasquelle, 1931.
An informative, copiously documented biography.

Bb69 Lejeune, Paule, *'Germinal': un roman antipeuple*, Nizet, 1978.
An uncompromisingly polemical work which seeks to show that, contrary to general assumptions, *Germinal* is fundamentally anti-proletarian, for both its structure and historical vision reflect Z's deep attachment to ruling-class ideology.

Lindenberg, Daniel, Jean-Pierre Vincent, Michel Deutsch and Jacques Blanc: see Bb44.

Bb70 Lloyd, Everett T., *The Evolution of the Attitude in the United States towards EZ*, New York U.P., 1949.
A brief monograph (18 pp.).

Bb71 Lorencini, Alvaro, *La Comparaison et la métaphore dans 'Germinal' d'EZ*, São Paulo: Faculdade de Filosofia, Ciências e Letras de Assis, 1972.
A penetrating analysis of the stylistic function of Z's images. Interesting for both substantive and methodological reasons.

Bb72 Louis, Paul, *Les Types sociaux chez Balzac et Z*, Edns du monde moderne, 1925.
A descriptive categorization.

Bb73 *Le Magazine littéraire*, 132 (Jan. 1978).

Bb74 Mallarmé, Stéphane, *Dix-neuf lettres de Stéphane Mallarmé à EZ*, ed. Léon Deffoux, La Centaine, 1929.

Mann, Heinrich: see Bc262.

Bb75 Martineau, Henri, *Le Roman scientifique d'EZ. La Médecine et 'Les Rougon-Macquart'*, Baillière, 1907.

Stresses the inadequacy of the medical documentation in Z's novels.

Bb76   Massis, Henri, *Comment EZ composait ses romans*, Fasquelle, 1906.
Based on Z's *notes de travail* for *L'Assommoir*, this book is the first of the genetic studies of individual novels. In need of extensive revision in the light of subsequent research.

Bb77   Matthews, J.H., *Les Deux Z. Science et personnalité dans l'expression*, Geneva: Droz, 1957.
A systematic demonstration (mainly by quotation rather than by close stylistic analysis) of the complementary and interdependent relationship between Z as scientific observer and visionary artist.

Bb78   Maupassant, Guy de, *EZ*, Quantin, 1883.
A brief, lyrical monograph (32 pp.).

Bb79   Max, Stefan, *Les Métamorphoses de la grande ville dans 'Les Rougon-Macquart'*, Nizet, 1966.
Eschewing any concern with the naturalistic qualities of Z's descriptions, perceptively examines the author's poetic and symbolic transformations of Paris, which becomes 'une sorte de Protée chargé des secrets et des angoisses de celui qui le décrit et de ceux qui le regardent' (p. 40). Discusses *La Curée, Le Ventre de Paris, L'Assommoir, L'Oeuvre, L'Argent* and (in an appendix) *Paris*. Comments on affinities with Dickens, the Impressionists, the Symbolists, the Surrealists and the *nouveau roman*. Cf. Bb63.

Bb80   Mitterand, Henri, *Z journaliste. De l'affaire Manet à l'affaire Dreyfus*, Armand Colin, 1962.
An excellent and all too brief synoptic account of Z's huge and varied journalistic output. Skilfully sets his journalism against its political and literary background and makes perceptive comments on the relationship between his journalism and his fiction. Contains a useful bibliography.

Bb81   ——, and Halina Suwala, *EZ journaliste. Bibliographie chronologique et analytique I (1859-1881)*, Les Belles Lettres, 1968.
Admirably meticulous and seemingly exhaustive, apart from the large number of unsigned articles published in *Le Sémaphore de Marseille* between 1871 and 1877 which are listed in Bb97. Includes details of short stories and poems.

Bb82   ——, and Jean Vidal, eds, *Album Z*, Gallimard, Bibliothèque de la Pléiade, 1963.
A kind of pictorial biography: contains 470 illustrations (including some

photographs taken by Z himself) which add up to an evocative portrait of Z and his age.

Bb83 Moreau, Pierre, *'Germinal' d'EZ, épopée et roman* (Les Cours de Sorbonne), Centre de documentation universitaire, 1954.
A mimeographed series of lectures. Contains an extensive bibliographical *préambule* and useful observations on the novel's epic aspects and narrative technique.

Bb84 *Le Naturalisme. Colloque de Cerisy*, ed. Pierre Cogny, Union générale d'édns (série 10/18), 1978.
Contains Bc93, 121, 139, 180, 400; Bd71, 293; Bf6, 56.

Bb85 Niess, Robert J., *Z, Cézanne, and Manet. A Study of 'L'Oeuvre'*, Ann Arbor: Univ. of Michigan Press, 1968.
Shorter than Bb14 but no less scholarly. The book is mainly concerned with the sources of the novel, but chapters are also devoted to its genesis, literary qualities and meaning. Much attention is given to the possible models of Claude Lantier: Niess concludes, like Brady, that the painter is largely a fictional composite of several individuals. Examines elements of self-projection in Z's portraits of Lantier and the novelist, Sandoz, and makes judicious observations on the relation of *L'Oeuvre* to the Impressionist movement (he vigorously contests Brady's contention that Claude is a Naturalist, not an Impressionist, arguing that for Z Impressionism and Naturalism were virtually synonymous terms), to Symbolism and to the current of intellectual pessimism in France in the late 19th century.

Bb86 Oehlert, Richard, *EZ als Theaterdichter mit einer Einleitung über den Naturalismus im französischen Drama*, Berlin: Ebering, 1920; repr. Nendeln-Liechtenstein: Kraus, 1967.

Bb87 Parturier, Maurice, *Z et Duranty (notes et documents)*, Giraud-Badin, 1948.

Bb88 Patterson, J.G., *A Z Dictionary. The Characters of the Rougon-Macquart Novels of EZ*, London: Routledge; New York: Dutton, 1912; repr. London: Routledge; Detroit: Gale, 1969, and New York: Georg Olms, 1973.
A useful handbook which provides summarized biographies of every character in *Les Rougon-Macquart*; the 1912 introduction (retained for the reprint) is very dated. Cf. Bb93.

Bb89 *Poétique*, 16 (1973) (Le discours réaliste).
Contains Bc120, 177; Bd196.

Bb90   *Présence de Z*, ed. Marc Bernard, Fasquelle, 1953.
Contains a large number of *témoignages* by French and foreign writers, together with articles under the headings, 'Z et la science et la sociologie' and 'Z et les arts, la médecine et la technique'; there are also some unpubd letters. Provides a good reflection of Z's reputation and influence. Includes Bc161, 206, 211, 212, 227, 260, 264, 334, 378, 384; Bd93, 317, 319; Be5; Bf17, 70; Bh19, 29.

Bb91   Proulx, Alfred C., *Aspects épiques des 'Rougon-Macquart' de Z*, The Hague: Mouton, 1966.
A careful but schematic examination of some central aspects of Z's themes and techniques (destiny, determinism, allegorical personification, repetition, symbolic imagery, the 'personnage-type') which seeks to show how closely Z's novels fit certain definitions of the epic in general (especially those of Hegel and Lascelles Abercrombie) and of the nineteenth-century French epic in particular (as described by H.J. Hunt). Useful but contains nothing new.

Bb92   Psichari, Henriette, *Anatomie d'un chef-d'oeuvre: 'Germinal'*, Mercure de France, 1964.
Provides less than its title promises, being a relatively cursory assessment of the novel's historicity. Includes a plot summary and selected extracts from the text.

Bb93   Ramond, F.C., *Les Personnages des 'Rougon-Macquart'. Pour servir à la lecture et à l'étude de l'oeuvre de Z*, Charpentier, 1901; repr. New York: Burt Franklin, 1970.
A useful guide which provides detailed biographical information and character sketches. Cf. Bb88.

Bb94   *Revue des sciences humaines*, 160 (1975) (Le Naturalisme).
Contains Bc17, 43, 116, 178, 363; Bd162; Bf32.

Bb95   *Revue de l'Université d'Ottawa/University of Ottawa Quarterly*, XLVIII, 4 (Oct.-Dec. 1978).
Largely devoted to Z's 'années d'apprentissage'. Contains Bc30, 90, 373; Bd136, 137, 244, 374; Be26; Bf78.

Bb96   Richardson, Joanna, *EZ*, London: Weidenfeld, 1978.
A workmanlike biography, but adds little to existing knowledge or appreciation. The book is restricted by the author's clear lack of feeling for Z and his work.

Bb97   Ripoll, Roger, *EZ journaliste. Bibliographie chronologique et*

analytique – II ('Le Sémaphore de Marseille', 1871-1877), Les Belles Lettres, 1972.
Cf. Bb81.

Bb98   Robert, Guy, *EZ. Principes et caractères généraux de son oeuvre*, Les Belles Lettres, 1952.
A sound introductory study which did much to rehabilitate Z's reputation and to show that he was a more conscious and complex artist than was often supposed. Contains chapters on the formation of Z's ideas on art, his theoretical writings, his methods of composition, the social themes of *Les Rougon-Macquart*, his use of myth, his narrative style and techniques, and the post-*Rougon-Macquart* novels. A defect of the book is that, by presenting Z's work as a static, monolithic whole, it fails to describe the ways in which it evolved.

Bb99   ——. *'La Terre' d'EZ. Etude historique et critique*, Les Belles Lettres, 1952.
A landmark in Z studies: a massive, scholarly analysis, making ample use of manuscript material kept at the Bibliothèque nationale, of the background, sources, genesis, themes, techniques and reception of *La Terre*. Paved the way for subsequent studies of individual novels (see Bb14, 37, 39, 47, 49, 60, 85, 120). Especially noteworthy for the pioneering investigation of mythical structures in Z's fiction.

——, ed.: see Bb29.

Bb100   Romains, Jules, *Z et son exemple*, Flammarion, 1935; repr. in *Saints de notre calendrier*, Flammarion, 1952, pp. 113-29.
A personal expression of admiration which stresses Z's status as a civic hero.

Bb101   Root, Winthrop H., *German Criticism of Z, 1875-1893*, New York: Columbia U.P., 1931.

Bb102   Rufener, Helen La Rue, *Biography of a War Novel: Z's 'La Débâcle'*, New York: King's Crown Press, 1946.
A somewhat superficial genetic study.

Bb103   Salvan, Albert J., *Z aux Etats-Unis*, Providence: Brown U.P., 1943; New York: Kraus Reprint Co., 1967.
A study of Z's reputation and influence in the United States.

Bb104   Schor, Naomi, *Z's Crowds*, Baltimore: The Johns Hopkins U.P., 1978.

A sophisticated and very stimulating study which draws on structural semantics, anthropology and psychoanalysis for its guiding concepts and working vocabulary, using the crowd as a structuring theme which engages all of Z's fiction.

Bb105 Serres, Michel, *Feux et signaux de brume: Z*, Grasset, 1975.
A difficult, but rich and challenging, global study which uses the methods of structuralist analysis to explore the thought patterns of Z's fiction and, through them, the modes of interaction between science and literature.

Bb106 Smethurst, Colin, *Z: 'Germinal'* (Studies in French Literature, 29), London: Edward Arnold, 1974.
An excellent introductory study. The first section deals succinctly with Z's conception of the Rougon-Macquart series, the genesis of *Germinal*, the author's use of documentation, and the *Ebauche*; the second section discusses the character of Etienne (this is particularly suggestive, pointing to the links between personal tensions and political behaviour, and to 'the need for a revaluation of Z as psychologist'), Z's presentation of working-class ideologies, his depiction of the bourgeois and working-class worlds, and the novel's mythical dimension.

Bb107 Suwala, Halina, *Naissance d'une doctrine. Formation des idées littéraires et esthétiques de Z (1859-1865)*, Univ. of Warsaw, 1976.
An extremely well-documented study — including a number of hitherto unpubd texts — of a decisive period in Z's development.

Bb108 Ten Brink, Jan, *EZ. Letterkundige Studie*, Nijmegen: Blomhert & Timmerman, 1879; revised edn: Leyden: Sythoff, 1884.
An enthusiastic study by the principal advocate in Holland of 'le roman scientifique'; cf. Bd52, 310.

Bb109 Ternois, René, *Z et son temps. 'Lourdes' — 'Rome' — 'Paris'*, Les Belles Lettres, 1961.
A monumental, many-faceted presentation of Z's reactions to the *fin-de-siècle* intellectual background.

Bb110 ——, *Z et ses amis italiens. Documents inédits*, Les Belles Lettres, 1967.

Bb111 Toulouse, Edouard, *Enquête médico-psychologique sur les rapports de la supériorité intellectuelle avec la névropathie. EZ*, Société d'édns scientifiques, 1896.

A detailed, often revealing, pre-Freudian analysis of Z's personality.

Bb112   Van Tieghem, Philippe, *Introduction à l'étude d'EZ: 'Germinal'*
(documents inédits de la Bibliothèque nationale) (Les Cours de
Sorbonne), Centre de documentation universitaire, 1954.
Mainly a description of the 'notes de travail'.

Bb113   Vial, André-Marc, *'Germinal' et le 'socialisme' de Z* (Coll. 'Les
Classiques du peuple. Critique'), Edns sociales, 1975.
An intelligent study of the circumstances of the novel's composition, its
social themes, and the contradictions in Z's ideology.

Bb114   Viens, Jacques, *'La Terre' de Z et 'Trente Arpents' de Ringuet.*
Etude comparée, Montreal: Edns Cosmos, 1970.

Bb115   Walker, Philip, *EZ* (Profiles in Literature), London: Routledge
& Kegan Paul, 1968.
A presentation of Z in specifically literary terms by means of short
extracts from the novels (in English tr.) accompanied by critical comments; naturally enough, there is much emphasis on the poetic aspects
of Z's talent. The extracts are consistently apt and the comments perti-
nent. There is also a useful annotated bibliography.

Bb116   Walter, Gerhard, *EZ. Der Deuter des 'Fin de Siècle'*, Munich:
Max Hueber, 1959.
Considers *Les Rougon-Macquart* chronologically.

Bb117   Williams, Merryn, *'Germinal'* (The Nineteenth-Century Novel
and its Legacy), Milton Keynes: The Open University Press,
1973 (39 pp.).

Bb118   Wilson, Angus, *EZ: An Introductory Study of his Novels,*
London: Secker & Warburg, 1952; revised 1964.
A stimulating biographical and critical study written from a broadly
Freudian point of view.

Bb119   *Yale French Studies*, 42 (1969).
Contains Bc6, 189, 272, 355, 389; Bd102, 140, 192, 295; Bf12, 63.
Nearly all of these articles are exercises in thematic criticism, drawing
upon the methods of *la nouvelle critique*.

Bb120   Zakarian, Richard H., *Z's 'Germinal'. A Critical Study of its*
Primary Sources, Geneva: Droz, 1972.
A scrupulous study of the factual basis of *Germinal* and the role of Z's

documentary sources in his imaginary universe. Concludes that the documentary content is both reliable and exhaustive, and that the relationship between documentation and imagination is complementary, dialectical and concurrent. More systematic and comprehensive than Bb37, 47, 92, 112.

Bb121   Zévaès, Alexandre, *A la gloire de ... Z*, Nouvelle Revue Critique, 1945.
A very sympathetic biographical study.

Bb122   ——, *Le Cinquantenaire de 'J'accuse!'*, Fasquelle, 1948.
A narrative account of Z's involvement in the Dreyfus Affair.

Bb123*   Zilli, L., *Z. Un approcio critico*, Milan: Editr. Viscontea, 1976.

Bb124   *Z* (Coll. 'Génies et Réalités'), Hachette, 1969.
A sumptuously illustrated collection of essays. Contains Bc202, 411; Bd3; Bf1; Bg24; Bh12.

SECTION Bc-h

Articles
(including books which contain sections on
or significant references to Z)

Bc   General

Bc1   Adam, Paul, 'Le maître du néant', *La Grande Revue*, I (Oct.
       1887), 172-8.

Bc2   Adhémar, Jean, 'La myopie d'EZ', *Aesculape*, n.s., XXXIII
       (1952), 194-7.
       The effect of myopia on Z's descriptions and artistic tastes.

Bc3   ——, 'De quelques sources iconographiques des romans de Z',
       in *EZ. Exposition organisée pour le cinquantième anniversaire
       de sa mort* (catalogue), Bibliothèque nationale, 1952, pp. xi-xiii.

Bc4   Ahnebrink, Lars, 'The Influence of Z', in *The Beginnings of
       Naturalism in American Fiction. A Study of the Works of Hame-
       lin Garland, Stephen Crane, and Frank Norris with Special Refer-
       ence to Some European Influences, 1891-1903*, Cambridge, Mass.:
       Harvard U.P., 1950, pp. 233-308.

       Alas, Leopoldo: see Bc79.

Bc5   Albalat, Antoine, 'Relations de Z avec Flaubert', in *Gustave
       Flaubert et ses amis*, Plon, 1927, pp. 233-40.

Bc6   Alcorn, Clayton R., Jr, 'The Child and his Milieu in the *Rougon-
       Macquart*', in Bb119, pp. 105-14.
       Argues that Z's children personify and reflect the spirit of the milieux he
       portrays, but overemphasizes the benign and protective influence of environ-
       ment.

Bc7   ——, 'The Domestic Servant in Z's Novels', in Bb32, pp. 21-35.

Bc8   Aragon, Louis, 'Actualité d'EZ', in *La Lumière de Stendhal*,

33

Denoël, 1954, pp. 245-57.
Text of a speech given at Médan on 29.9.46; argues that the importance of Z's moral and political 'example' should not be forgotten, for the tendencies embodied in *anti-Dreyfusisme* led directly to Vichy and the near-destruction of France.

Bc9 Armstrong, Judith, Refs in *The Novel of Adultery*, London: Macmillan, 1976.
Sexual patterns in *Thérèse Raquin*, *Une Page d'amour*, *Nana*, *Pot-Bouille* and *La Bête humaine*.

Bc10 Arrighi, Paul, Refs in *Le Vérisme dans la prose narrative italienne*, Boivin, 1937.

Bc11 ——, 'Z en Italie: Z et De Sanctis', *RLC*, XXVII (1953), 438-46.
Cf. Bc38, 107; Bd24.

Bc12 Auriant, L., 'Un disciple anglais [*sic*] d'EZ: George Moore', *NF*, CCXCVII (1940), 312-23.

Bc13 Baguley, David, 'Image et symbole: la tache rouge dans l'oeuvre de Z', *CN*, 39 (1970), 36-41.
Examines the recurrent image of 'la tache rouge' up to *La Bête humaine* as a symbol of crime and guilt; distinguishes between a conscious, allegorical use of the image and a less deliberate, symbolic use which persistently links love and guilt and probably springs from Z's personal preoccupations concerning sexuality.

Bc14 ——, 'Les oeuvres de Z traduites en anglais (1878-1968)', *CN*, 40 (1970), 195-209.

Bc15 ——, 'L'anti-intellectualisme de Z', *CN*, 42 (1971), 119-29.
Despite Z's rationalism and his powerful portrayal of the destructive capacity of man's instinctive urges, he distrusted pure intellectualism and remained deeply sceptical of absolute attachment to any ideology.

Bc16 Bakker, B.H., ed., 'Vingt-cinq lettres inédites de Paul Alexis à EZ et à Jeanne Rozerot (1890-1900)', *CN*, 49 (1975), 30-63.
Cf. Bb7.

Bc17 ——, 'Z aux Pays-Bas, 1875-1885: contribution à l'étude du naturalisme européen', in Bb94, pp. 581-8.

Bc18 Bange, Pierre, 'Fontane et le naturalisme. Une critique inédite des *Rougon-Macquart*', *Etudes germaniques*, XIX (1964), 142-64;

partially repr. in Theodor Fontane, *Schriften und Glossen zur europäischen Literatur* (Klassiker der Kritik), I, ed. Werner Weber, Zürich: Artemis, 1965, pp. 201-18.
Fontane's reflections on *La Fortune des Rougon* and *La Conquête de Plassans* (part of his plans for a projected essay on Z).

Bc19   Barjon, Louis, 'Le monde du réalisme. EZ', in *Mondes d'écrivains – destinées d'hommes*, Castermann, 1960, pp. 15-30.

Bc20   Barrès, Maurice, 'Maurice Barrès et Z', in *L'Oeuvre de Maurice Barrès*, ed. Philippe Barrès, Club de l'Honnête Homme, 1965, IV, pp. 603-29.
Concerning Barrès's opposition to the transfer of Z's ashes to the Panthéon.

Bc21   Barry, Catherine A., Refs in *'La Revue des Deux Mondes* in Transition: From the Death of Naturalism to the Early Debate on Literary Cosmopolitanism', *MLR*, LXVIII (1973), 545-50.

Bc22   Basdekis, Demetrios, 'Unamuno and Z: Notes on the Novel', *MLN*, LXXXVIII (1973), 366-74.
Unamuno's critical reactions to Z's Naturalism seen in the context of the former's progressive abandonment of the aesthetics of objective realism.

Bc23   Baudson, Pierre, 'Z et la caricature, d'après les recueils Céard du musée Carnavalet', *CN*, 29 (1965), 43-60.

Bc24   ——, 'Les romans de Z et la caricature de leur temps', *Gazette des Beaux-Arts*, 1328 (1979), 69-94.
158 illustrations from the period 1868-97, preceded by a short introduction.

Bc25   Becker, Colette, 'Du garni à l'hôtel particulier: quelques aperçus sur la vie et l'oeuvre de Z à partir des calepins cadastraux', *CN*, 43 (1972), 1-24.
Insights into Z's poverty-stricken early years in Paris.

Bc26   ——, 'François Z et son fils', *CN*, 44 (1972), 136-57.
Valuable information on Z's father and his relationship with his son.

Bc27   ——, 'L'audience d'EZ', *CN*, 47 (1974), 40-69.
An admirably thorough enquiry into the nature of Z's nineteenth-century readership.

Bc28   ——, 'Un professeur de Z: Pierre-Emile Levasseur. Sur quelques problèmes posés par les lettres de jeunesse de l'écrivain', *CN*, 49

(1975), 68-82.

Bc29 ——, 'Z et *Le Travail* (1862)', *CN*, 51 (1977), 109-19.
Shows how Z's dealings with this short-lived review shed light on his early intellectual development.

Bc30 ——, 'Z à la librairie Hachette', in Bb95, pp. 287-309.

Bc31 Bell, David, 'Serres' Z: Literature, Science, Myth', *MLN*, XCIV (1979), 797-808.
An incisive explication of Bb105.

Bc32 Bellet, R., 'Une correspondance Vallès-Z (1865-1879)', *Europe*, 470-2 (1968), 171-81.

Bc33 Berteaux, Félix, 'L'influence de Z en Allemagne', *RLC*, IV (1924), 73-91.

Bc34 Bertrand-Jennings, Chantal, 'Le conquérant zolien: de l'arriviste au héros mythique', *Romantisme*, 23 (1979), 43-53.
Traces the metamorphoses of 'le conquérant' from the Abbé Faujas (*La Conquête de Plassans*) to Luc Froment (*Travail*), locating the transition from 'arriviste' to 'héros mythique' in the figure of Pascal Rougon (*Le Docteur Pascal*).

——: see also Jennings, Chantal, Bc207; Bd267-9, 347.

Bc35 Bettinson, C.D., and L.J. Newton, 'Gide, Z and the Legacy of Naturalism in *Les Caves du Vatican*', *Neophilologus*, LX (1976), 200-6.
Argue that *Les Caves du Vatican* both reflects and parodies the behaviourist theories of Z.

Bc36 Blasco Ibáñez, Vicente, 'EZ', in *Discursos literarios*, Valencia: Prometeo, 1966, pp. 137-62.
A lecture delivered in 1909. Cf. Bc137.

Bc37 Blaze de Bury, Fernande, 'The Mythology of the Nineteenth Century. M. EZ', *Scottish Review*, XXXV (1900), 89-105.
A perceptive early critique of Z's scientific pretensions; assesses Z as a 'lyrical poet' rather than a realist.

Bc38 Bonfantini, Mario, 'De Sanctis e Z', *Rivista di Letterature Moderne e Comparate* (Florence), XIX (1966), 183-8.
Cf. Bc11, 107; Bd24.

Bc39   Bonnefis, Philippe, 'Le bestiaire d'EZ. Valeur et signification des images animales dans son oeuvre romanesque', in Bb34, pp. 97-107; repr. in Ba12, pp. 117-29.

Bc40   ——, 'Situation chronologique et textuelle de *Printemps — Journal d'un convalescent*', *CN*, 39 (1970), 1-35.

Bc41   ——, 'Le descripteur mélancolique', in *La Description. Nodier, Sue, Flaubert, Hugo, Verne, Z, Alexis, Fénéon*, Lille: Edns universitaires, 1974, pp. 103-51.
A study of the relations between Naturalist notions of Life and Death and the death-instinct.

Bc42   ——, 'Fluctuations de l'image, en régime naturaliste', *RSH*, 154 (1974), 283-300.
Structuralist discussion of Z's art criticism and of pictorial elements in his fiction.

Bc43   ——, 'Le cri de l'étain', in Bb94, pp. 513-38.
Structuralist analysis of Oedipal patterns and the themes of the machine, birth and heredity in Z's fiction; cf Bb13.

Bc44   ——, Refs in 'Intérieurs naturalistes', in *Intime, intimité, intimisme*, ed. R. Molho and P. Reboul, Univ. de Lille III: Edns universitaires, 1976, pp. 163-98.

Bc45   ——, 'Hydrographies naturalistes', *CN*, 50 (1976), 213-23.
Manifold forms of liquidity in Z seen in a mythical perspective. Cf. Bc159; Bd102.

Bc46   Bordier, Roger, 'Sur Z et Proust. L'esprit de famille, l'art et le réel', *Europe*, 496-7 (1970), 218-28.
A schematic comparative study.

Bc47   Borie, Jean, Review of Bb34, *RHLF*, LXXI (1971), 116-21.

Bc48   Boulier, Jean, '*Les Trois Villes*: *Lourdes, Rome, Paris*', in Bb34, pp. 135-46.

Bc49   Bourget, Paul, 'Le roman réaliste et le roman piétiste', *RDM*, CVI (1873), 454-69 (pp. 456-60).
Hostile comments, based on the first three volumes of *Les Rougon-Macquart*, on Z's style, vulgarity and materialism ('dès l'abord M. Z nous apparaît comme un homme pour qui le monde intérieur n'existe pas').

Bc50   Bourneuf, Roland, and Réal Ouellet, Refs in *L'Univers du roman*,
        P.U.F., 1972.
        Useful remarks in the context of a stimulating introduction to problems in
        the technique of the novel.

Bc51   Braescu, Ion, 'Z vu par Barbusse', *Europe*, 545 (1974), 151-6.

Bc52   Braibant, Charles, 'Anatole France et Z', in *Le Secret d'Anatole
        France*, Denoël & Steele, 1935, pp. 285-302.

Bc53   Brown, Calvin S., 'Music in Z's Fiction, especially Wagner's Music',
        PMLA, LXXI (1956), 84-96.
        Music considered as a source of techniques as well as subject-matter. Cf.
        Bb16; Bc54, 82, 171, 251.

Bc54   ——, and Robert J. Niess, 'Wagner and Z again', *PMLA*, LXXIII
        (1958), 448-52.
        Niess contests Brown's argument that Z's technique of repetition could not
        have been inspired by a similar technique in Wagner's music. Cf. Bb16; Bc53,
        82, 171, 251.

Bc55   Bruneau, Charles, 'EZ [1840-1902]', in Ferdinand Brunot, *Hist-
        oire de la langue française des origines à nos jours*, XIII, deuxième
        partie, Armand Colin, 1972, pp. 141-63.
        A schematic account of Z's style.

Bc56   Brunetière, Ferdinand, *Le Roman naturaliste*, Calmann Lévy,
        1882; revised 1892. (The 1882 edn contains 'Le roman réaliste
        en 1875' [pp. 1-29], *'Le Roman expérimental'* [pp. 105-35] , 'Les
        origines du roman naturaliste' [pp. 243-70] and Bd305; the 1892
        edn contains Bd324.)
        Attacks Z for his naïve scientific pretensions, narrowness of vision, lack of
        psychological penetration and persistent obscenity. It has been plausibly
        suggested (see Bb13 and Bc315) that these attacks mask bourgeois fear of
        the politically seditious nature of Z's fiction. Cf. Bb36.

Bc57   Burns, Colin A., 'EZ et Henry Céard', *CN*, 2 (1955), 81-7.

Bc58   ——, 'Z et l'Angleterre', *CN*, 12 (1959), 495-503.

Bc59   ——, 'Z in Exile. Notes on an Unpublished Diary of 1898', *FS*,
        XVII (1963), 14-26.

Bc60   ——, 'Documentation et imagination chez EZ', *CN*, 24-5 (1963),
        69-78.

Stresses the organic relationship between documentation and imagination in Z.

Bc61   Butor, Michel, 'Z', in *Tableau de la littérature française*, III. *De Madame de Staël à Rimbaud*, Gallimard, 1974, pp. 360-7.

Bc62   Cantoni, Edda, 'Letteratura e politica nel secondo ottocento francese: Z e Vallès', *Rivista di Letterature Moderne e Comparate* (Florence), XVII (1964), 215-32.

Bc63   Carias, Léon, 'France et Z avant l'Affaire', *La Grande Revue*, CXXIV (1927), 402-38.

Bc64   Carrère, Jean, 'EZ', in *Les Mauvais Maîtres*, Plon, 1922, pp. 199-233.
The power and unity of Z's work is marred by a pernicious narrowness of vision, concentration on 'laideurs morales', and a demoralizing pessimism.

Bc65   Carter, A.E., Refs in *The Idea of Decadence in French Literature, 1830-1900*, Univ. of Toronto Press, 1958 (esp. pp. 71-81).
On the themes of degeneracy and neurosis in Z. Suggests that 'the most interesting thing about Z's conception of decadence is that it shows an evolution characteristic of the time: it begins as something literary and aesthetic (his essays on Taine and the Goncourts), acquires a medical and scientific tone from his readings in psychopathology, and ends in a revival of the nature-cult (*Fécondité*)'; concludes, however, that the theme of degeneracy in Z, 'while it touches decadence at so many points, is not self-conscious enough to be truly decadent'. Cf. Bc136.

Bc66   Cassaing, Jean-Claude, 'La vengeance de la vérité', *CN*, 51 (1977), 18-34.
On the subversive nature of Z's depiction of social injustice and class divisions.

Bc67   Cazaux, Michèle, 'Z en Suède', *RLC*, XXVII (1953), 428-37.

Bc68   Céard, Henry, 'Z intime', *Revue illustrée*, III (1887), 141-8; repr. in *Bulletin de la Société littéraire des amis de Z*, 6 (1925), 40-5.
Useful account of Z's personality, temperament and tastes, and his life at Médan.

Bc69   Céline, Louis-Ferdinand, 'Hommage à EZ', *Bulletin de la Société littéraire des amis de Z*, 18 (1933), 10-14.

Cézanne, Paul: see Bc327.

Bc70 Chabaud, Alfred, 'Un épisode inconnu de l'enfance d'EZ', *MF*, CCX (1929), p. 508.

A Marseilles police report of April 1845 records the arrest of a twelve-year-old Algerian boy accused of indecent conduct with the five-year-old Z; this incident, which Z himself never alluded to, may presumably have influenced Z's later feelings of guilt concerning sexuality.

Bc71 Chartreux, Bernard, 'Après *Germinal*', in Bb44, pp. 39-50.

A perceptive analysis of the basic themes of *Les Quatre Evangiles*. Stresses the importance of these novels for a global understanding of Z's work.

Bc72 Chennevière, Georges, 'EZ', *Europe*, 60 (1927), 504-23; 61 (1928), 85-102.

A perceptive essay written (in praise of Z) in 1908.

Bc73 Chevrel, Yves, 'Les relations de Z avec le monde germanique', *CN*, 46 (1973), 227-47.

Bc74 ——, 'EZ et le métier d'écrivain', *CN*, 53 (1979), 19-28.

Bc75 Christie, John, 'Naturalisme et naturisme: les relations d'EZ avec Saint-Georges de Bouhélier et Maurice Leblond', *NFS*, II (Oct. 1963), 11-24.

Bc76 ——, 'Z and Bouhélier: Their Times and Relationship, Based on the Unpublished Correspondence of Saint-Georges de Bouhélier', *NFS*, VIII (Oct. 1969), 83-100.

Bc77 ——, 'An Interview with EZ: An Unpublished Manuscript by Saint-Georges de Bouhélier', *NFS*, XI (Oct. 1972), 45-52.

Bc78 Citron, Pierre, 'Quelques aspects romantiques du Paris de Z', *CN*, 24-5 (1963), 47-54.

Z's portrayal of Paris in the first nine *Rougon-Macquart* novels. Cf. Bc89, 409.

Bc79 Clarín [Leopoldo Alas], 'La juventud literaria', in *Ensayos y revistas 1888-1892*, Madrid: Manuel Fernández y Lasanta, 1892, pp. 393-7.

A critique of Z's negative attitude towards idealist currents in the novel.

Bc80 Claverie, Michel, 'La fête impériale', *CN*, 45 (1973), 31-49.

The tonality of Second Empire life as reflected in *Les Rougon-Macquart*.

Bc81 Cocteau, Jean, 'Z, le poète', *CN*, 11 (1958), 442-3.

Bc82 Coeuroy, André, 'Le naturalisme', in *Wagner et l'esprit roman-
tique*, Gallimard, 1965, pp. 287-301.
Mainly on *Le Ventre de Paris* and *La Faute de l'abbé Mouret*. Cf. Bb16;
Bc53, 54, 171, 251.

Bc83 Cogny, Pierre, ed., 'Les lettres inédites d'Edmond de Goncourt à
EZ', *CN*, 13 (1959), 526-42.

Bc84 ——, 'EZ devant le problème de Jésus-Christ, d'après des docu-
ments inédits', *Studi Francesi*, VIII (1964), 255-64.
Z's notes (taken in about 1900) on various works on religion (notably
Renan's *Vie de Jésus*) show a surprising degree of sympathy for Christianity.

Bc85 ——, 'Z évangéliste', in Bb34, pp. 147-51.
On the thematic continuity between *Les Quatre Evangiles* and the rest of
Z's work.

Bc86 ——, 'Z républicain', in *L'Esprit républicain* (Colloque d'Orléans,
4 et 5 septembre 1970), Klincksieck, 1972, pp. 353-8.
Z's conception of the Republic from his first newspaper articles and *La
Fortune des Rougon* to the Dreyfus Affair.

Bc87 Colburn, William E., 'Victorian Translations of Z', *Studies in the
Literary Imagination* (Georgia State College), I (1968), 23-32.

Bc88 Collet, Georges-Paul, 'George Moore et EZ' and 'L'influence de
Z', in *George Moore et la France,* Geneva: Droz, 1957, pp. 19-22,
122-47.

Bc89 Cornell, Kenneth, 'Z's City', *Yale French Studies*, 32 (1964),
106-11.
Z's portrayal of Paris in *Les Rougon-Macquart*. Cf. Bc78.

Bc90 Couillard, M., 'La "fille-fleur" dans *Les Contes à Ninon* et *Les
Rougon-Macquart*', in Bb95, pp. 398-406.

Bc91 Croce, Benedetto, 'Z e Daudet', in *Poesia e non poesia. Note sulla
letteratura europea de secolo decimonono*, Bari: Laterza, 1923,
pp. 279-90.
A less favourable view of Z than that proposed by De Sanctis in Bc107: Z's
social vision is deficient, his scientism superannuated, and his imaginative
powers limited. Cf. Geoffrey E. Hare, *Alphonse Daudet: A Critical Bibliography*, II. *Secondary Material* (Research Bibliographies and Checklists, 24),
London: Grant & Cutler, 1979, Bb492 (see also his Bb922, 947, 1540).

Bc92 Dahlström, C., 'Strindberg's 'Naturalistiska Sorgespel' and Z's Naturalism', *Scandinavian Studies*, XVII (1943), 269-81; XVIII (1944-45), 14-36, 41-60, 98-114, 138-55, 183-94.

Bc93 Dallenbach, Lucien,'"L'oeuvre dans l'oeuvre"chez Z', in Bb84, pp. 125-39.
On Z's use of *mise en abyme* techniques.

Bc94 Dangelzer, Joan-Yvonne, 'Le milieu chez Z' in *La Description du milieu dans le roman français de Balzac à Z*, Les Presses modernes, 1938, pp. 193-248.

Bc95 Daudet, Léon, 'La bêtise de Z', in *Une Campagne d'Action française*, Nouvelle Librairie nationale, 1910, pp. 61-5.
Abuse directed against Z's allegedly manifold simple-mindedness.

Bc96 ——, 'Le naturalisme de Z', in *Fantômes et vivants. Souvenirs des milieux littéraires, politiques, artistiques et médicaux de 1880 à 1905*, Nouvelle Librairie nationale, 1914, pp. 53-60.
Valuable personal reminiscences: Z's personality, temperament and influence.

Bc97 ——, 'Le Z maigre', in *Devant la Douleur. Souvenirs des milieux littéraires, politiques, artistiques et médicaux de 1880 à 1905 (deuxième série)*, Nouvelle Librairie nationale, 1915, pp. 103-16.

Bc98 ——, 'Le cas de Z', in *Au Temps de Judas. Souvenirs des milieux littéraires, politiques, artistiques et médicaux de 1880 à 1908 (cinquième série)*, Nouvelle Librairie nationale, 1920, pp. 56-64.
'Z avait l'imagination odorante et sexuelle, mais courte'; the volume is largely an *anti-Dreyfusard* tract.

Bc99 ——, 'EZ ou le romantisme de l'égout', in *Les Oeuvres dans les hommes*, Nouvelle Librairie nationale, 1922, pp. 91-141.
Sustained abuse: *le zolisme* defined as a 'caricature obscène du romantisme'.

Bc100 Davis, Gifford, 'Catholicism and Naturalism: Pardo Bazán's Reply to Z', *MLN*, XC (1975), 282-7.
On Pardo Bazán's proudly acquiescent response (in the preface to the 1891 edn of *La cuestión palpitante*) to Z's expressed opinion that she could be only an artistic and formalistic follower of Naturalism because, as a Catholic, she would be unable to accept his materialist doctrines; although acknowledging Z's superiority as an author, Pardo Bazán claims that her brand of Naturalism is broader and more human than his. Cf. Bf61.

Bc101   De Amicis, Edmondo, 'EZ', in *Ricordi di Parigi*, Milan: Treves, 1879, pp. 213-90.
Records revelations by Z about his life and working methods.

Bc102   Decker, Clarence R., 'Z's Literary Reputation in England', *PMLA*, XLIX (1934), 1140-53.

Bc103   ——, 'The Aesthetic Revolt against Naturalism in Victorian Criticism', *PMLA*, LIII (1938), 844-56.

Bc104   Deffoux, Léon, 'EZ et la sous-préfecture de Castelsarrasin en 1871', *MF*, CXCI (1926), 336-46.

Bc105   ——, and Emile Zavie, *Le Groupe de Médan*, Payot, 1920 (esp. 'EZ, ou "je jette le gant" ', pp. 21-50).

Bc106   De Luca,Giuseppe, 'Ah, quell'udienza! – EZ e Leone XIII', *Nuova Antologia*, CDXXXIII (1945), 57-61.
On Z's abortive attempt to obtain an audience with Leo XIII in 1894.

Bc107   De Sanctis, Francesco, 'Studio sopra EZ', in *Saggi critici*, ed. Luigi Russo, 3 vols, Bari: Laterza, 1952, vol. III, pp. 234-76; repr. in *Il Manifesto del realismo*, ed. Rino Dal Sasso, Rome: Editori riuniti, 1972, pp. 33-89.
Written in 1877; a sympathetic general study of Z's work up to *Le Ventre de Paris*. Cf. Bc11, 38; Bd24.

Bc108   Descaves, Pierre, 'Le président Z', in Bb33, pp. 34-8.
On Z's contribution to La Société des gens de lettres.

Bc109   Desprez, Louis, 'EZ', in *L'Evolution naturaliste*, Tresse, 1884, pp. 177-261.
Cf. Bb29.

Bc110   Dezalay, Auguste, 'Z et le rêve', *TLLS*, VI (1968), 177-83.
Establishes the ambivalent theme of dream as 'une constante de l'univers de Z'.

Bc111   ——, 'Le thème du souterrain chez Z', in Bb34, pp. 110-21; partially repr. in Ba12, pp. 129-34.
Illustrates the multiplicity of forms assumed by the theme without attempting any synthesis. Cf. Bc114, 272; Bd208.

Bc112   ——, 'Pour déchiffrer Z: du goût des symétries à l'obsession des nombres', *TLLS*, VII (1969), 157-66.

Symmetrical patterns in the structure of Z's novels reflect a neurotic *arithmomanie* (cf. Bb111); numerical calculations assume increasing importance in his final works.

Bc113 ——, 'Le moteur immobile: Z et ses paralytiques', *TLLS*, VIII (1970), 63-74.
Z's paralytics (Mme Raquin in *Thérèse Raquin*, Tante Dide in *La Fortune des Rougon* and *Le Docteur Pascal*, Chanteau in *La Joie de vivre*, Bonnemort in *Germinal*, Tante Phasie in *La Bête humaine*, Marie de Guersaint in *Lourdes*, Jérôme Qurignon in *Travail*, Achille in *Vérité*) function structurally as 'points fixes dans le tournoiement autour d'eux des intérêts et des passions' and symbolically as embodiments of permanence and fatality.

Bc114 ——, 'Le fil d'Ariane: de l'image à la structure du labyrinthe', *CN*, 40 (1970), 121-34.
Studies the transformations of the motif from *Madeleine Férat* to *Travail*. Cf. Bc111, 272.

Bc115 ——, 'L'exigence de totalité chez un romancier expérimental: Z face aux philosophes et aux classificateurs', in Bb19, pp. 167-84.

Bc116 ——, 'Les mystères de Z', in Bb94, pp. 475-87.
A suggestive analysis of the ways in which *Les Rougon-Macquart* 'se lisent comme des contes de fées'.

Bc117 Digeon, Claude, *La Crise allemande de la pensée française (1970-1914)*, P.U.F., 1959, pp. 271-87.
Sketches the evolution of Z's ideas on national regeneration from his stress in *Lettre à la jeunesse* and *La Débâcle* on the need for 'l'esprit scientifique' to the 'patriotisme idéaliste' of his final years.

Bc118 Dubois, Jacques, Refs in *Romanciers français de l'instantané au XIXe siècle*, Brussels: Palais des Académies, 1963.
On techniques used by Z to capture fleeting impressions.

Bc119 ——, 'Représentations de Z chez un public d'aujourd'hui. Résultats d'enquête', in Bb34, pp. 257-66.
An enquiry into conceptions of Z among a group of 98 Belgian tradeunionists.

Bc120 ——, 'Surcodage et protocole de lecture', in Bb89, pp. 491-18.
An analysis of the opening sentences of the Rougon-Macquart novels with

a view to demonstrating the highly artificial nature of 'realist' texts. Cf. Bc123, 127; Bd157.

Bc121 ——, 'Emergence et position du groupe naturaliste dans l'institution littéraire', in Bb84, pp. 75-91.

Bc122 Dubuc, André, 'Une amitié littéraire: Gustave Flaubert et EZ', *CN*, 28 (1964), 129-36.

A warm and lasting friendship; Flaubert admired Z's literary talent but expressed distaste for his theorizing: 'Le tort de Z, c'est d'avoir un système, de vouloir faire une école'.

Bc123 Duchet, Claude, 'Le monde et le texte dans les premières phrases des *Rougon-Macquart*', *Dossiers pédagogiques de la R.T.S.*, I (français, premier et second cycles, 1973-4), 49-59.

On the textual function of the opening sentences of the *Rougon-Macquart* novels. Cf. Bc120, 127; Bd157.

Bc124 Dumesnil, René, Refs in *L'Epoque réaliste et naturaliste*, Tallandier, 1945.

An informative account of French literary life in the second half of the nineteenth century.

Bc125 Duncan, Phillip A., 'Z's Machine-Monsters', *Romance Notes*, III (Spring 1962), 10-12.

Argues that Z's melodramatic portrayal of machines as devouring monsters in such novels as *Germinal* and *La Bête humaine* does not correspond to his belief in science and technology as essential agents of human progress but reflects certain stylistic preoccupations: animated machine-symbols become an element in the poetic expression of his positivist cosmography, reveal his liking for gothic effects, and serve as powerful focal points for action and themes. Cf. Bb13 (pp. 76-124); Bc306.

Bc126 ——, 'Echoes of Z's Experimental Novel in Russia', *Slavic and East European Journal*, XVIII (1974), 11-19.

On the profound influence of Z's 'scientific' theories on Russian literary polemics in the 1890s.

Bc127 Dupuy, Aimé, 'Les "entrées en matière" de Z', in Bb33, pp. 55-61.

On the differing techniques of Z and Balzac. Cf. Bc120, 123; Bd157.

Bc128 ——, 'Comment Z a vu et jugé Napoléon III', *Le Miroir de l'histoire*, 37 (1953), 81-4.

The presentation of Napoleon III in *La Curée*, *Son Excellence Eugène Rougon* and *La Débâcle*.

Bc129   ——, 'Autour des personnages de Z. Hommes politiques, fonctionnaires et magistrats dans *les Rougon-Macquart*', *Revue socialiste*, 64 (1953), 173-91.
The novels considered (from the point of view of their documentary and representational value) are *La Fortune des Rougon*, *La Curée*, *La Conquête de Plassans*, *Pot-Bouille*, *L'Argent*, *La Bête humaine* and (especially) *Son Excellence Eugène Rougon*.

Bc130   ——, 'Le Second Empire vu et jugé par EZ', *L'Information historique*, XV (March-April 1953), 50-7.
Praises the historical value of Z's work.

Bc131   Edwards, Herbert, 'Z and the American Critics', *American Literature* (Durham, N. Carolina), IV (1932), 114-29.

Bc132   Ehrard, Antoinette, 'EZ et Gustave Doré', *Gazette des Beaux-Arts*, 1238 (1972), 185-92.

Bc133   Ellis, Havelock, 'Z: The Man and his Work', in *Affirmations*, London: Constable, 1898, pp. 131-57.

Bc134   Ernst, Fritz, 'Der Dichter der *Rougon-Macquart*', in *Aus Goethes Freundeskreis und andere Essays*, Berlin: Suhrkamp, 1955, pp. 189-209.

Bc135   Esper, Erich, 'Schopenhauer in der Familie Les Rougon-Macquart', *Schopenhauer-Jahrbuch*, XXXIX (1958), 183-7.

Bc136   Esteban, Manuel A., 'Z's Democratization of the Concept of Decadence', *Degré second, 3 (July 1979), 109-32.*
A survey of Z's relations with the *décadents*, pointing out that although Z's work contains many decadent themes, he regarded decadence as a general social and historical phenomenon and not exclusively an aesthetic one as claimed by many a decadent. Cf. Bc65.

Bc137   ——, 'Z and Blasco Ibáñez: A New Look', *NCFS*, VIII (1979-80), 87-100.
Cf. Bc36.

Bc138   Fabre, F.-E., 'Jules Vallès et le naturalisme', *CN*, 8-9 (1957), 382-5.

Bc139   Falconer, Graham, 'Sagesse et folie de l'écriture zolienne', in Bb84, pp. 171-88.
Suggests ways in which Z invites his readers to play a more active role than has generally been assumed.

Bc140   Fischer, Ernst, *Von der Notwendigkeit der Kunst*, Dresden: Verlag der Kunst, 1959; English tr.: *The Necessity of Art: A Marxist Approach*, tr. Anna Bostock, Harmondsworth: Penguin Books, 1963 (see 'Naturalism', pp. 76-8).
Stresses the problematic nature of Naturalism, i.e., 'there comes a moment of decision when naturalism must either break through to socialism or founder in fatalism, symbolism, mysticism, religiosity, and reaction. Z chose the former path' (but only at the end of his career).

Bc141   Flaubert, Gustave, Refs in *Correspondance* (vols XII-XVI of *Oeuvres complètes*, 16 vols, Club de l'honnête homme, 1971-5).

Bc142   France, Anatole, 'Variétés. Les romanciers contemporains. M. EZ', *Le Temps* (27.6.1877).

Bc143   ——, Refs in *Vers les temps meilleurs. Trente ans de vie sociale*, ed. Claude Aveline and Henriette Psichari, 4 vols, Geneva: Editoservice, 1971.
These vols cover the years 1897-1904 (I), 1905-1908 (II), 1909-1914 (III), 1915-1924 (IV); the refs are numerous (but none in vol. IV). Vol. I (pp. 149-53) contains France's celebrated funeral oration of 5 Oct. 1902 ('il fut un moment de la conscience humaine').

Bc144   Fraser, Elizabeth M., Refs in *Le Renouveau religieux d'après le roman français de 1886 à 1914*, Les Belles Lettres, 1934.
Brief refs to the post-*Rougon-Macquart* works, seen in a broad intellectual context.

Bc145   Frierson, William C., *L'Influence du naturalisme français sur les romanciers anglais de 1885 à 1900*, Marcel Giard, 1925, *passim*.

Bc146   ——, Refs in 'The English Controversy over Realism in Fiction (1885-1895)', *PMLA*, XLIII (1928), 533-50.

Bc147   ——, and Herbert Edwards, Refs in 'Impact of French Naturalism on American Critical Opinion (1877-1892)', *PMLA*, LXIII (1948), 1007-16.

Bc148   Furst, Lilian R., 'George Moore et Z: une réévaluation', *CN*, 41 (1971), 42-57; repr. as 'George Moore, Z, and the Question of Influence', *Canadian Review of Comparative Literature/ Revue canadienne de littérature comparée*, I (1974), 138-55.
A judicious reassessment of Z's influence; suggests that there was no really deep or lasting influence from Z to Moore because there are too many reservations to make about their relationship.

Bc149   Gauthier, E. Paul, 'Z's Literary Reputation in Russia Prior to *L'Assommoir*', *FR*, XXXIII (1959-60), 37-44.

Bc150   ——, 'Z as Imitator of Flaubert's Style', *MLN*, LXXV (1960), 423-7.

Bc151   ——, 'New Light on Z and Physiognomy', *PMLA*, LXXV (1960), 297-308.

Bc152   Gauthier, Guy, 'Z et les images', in Bb34, pp. 400-16.
A study of Z's 'univers visuel' which identifies the ways in which his techniques prefigure the cinema; a filmography is appended (pp. 416-24). Cf. Bc206, 344; Bd191, 201, 326; Bf12.

Bc153   Gide, André, Refs in *Journal, 1889-1939*, and *Journal, 1939-1949*, Gallimard (Bibliothèque de la Pléiade), 1948 and 1954.
Some perceptive and appreciative observations by the author who wrote in 1932: 'Je tiens le discrédit actuel de Z pour une monstrueuse injustice, qui ne fait pas grand honneur aux critiques littéraires d'aujourd'hui.'

Bc154   Gingell, E., 'The Theme of Fertility in Z's *Rougon-Macquart*', *FMLS*, XIII (1977), 350-8.
Focuses on the tension between Z's view of procreation as natural and virtuous and his portrayal of a society unfit to receive children.

Bc155   Girard, Marcel, 'Z visionnaire', *Montjoie*, I, 2 (1953), 6-9.
'Il a fait entrer en lui le monde extérieur, et celui-ci n'en ressort par sa plume que chargé d'un pouvoir symbolique ou mythique.'

Bc156   ——, 'Naturalisme et symbolisme', *CAIEF*, VI (1954), 97-106.

Bc157   ——, 'Positions politiques d'EZ jusqu'à l'Affaire Dreyfus', *Revue française de science politique*, V (1955), 503-28.
A helpful survey which concludes that the only pattern discernible in Z's political attitudes and involvements is that 'il a épousé à peu près l'évolution de son temps, avec seulement assez d'avance sur l'opinion moyenne pour qu'on ait le droit de le considérer comme un homme de gauche';

usefully places Z's politics in the context of his literary milieu and pre-occupations.

Bc158 ——, 'EZ et Louise Solari', *RHLF*, LVIII (1958), 371-2.
Remarks on the hypothesis of an adolescent infatuation advanced by Lanoux in Bb64, pp. 33-5, 107. Cf. Bc185, 195.

Bc159 ——, 'Les "baignades" d'EZ', in Bb19, pp. 95-111.
Argues that Z's childhood *parties de campagne* on the banks of the Arc with Cézanne and Baille were more significant than Z's biographers have realised, for they made an indelible impression on his personality and fiction, in which 'le thème de l'eau s'orchestre en des pages innombrables, où chantent alternativement l'amour, le sommeil, la rêverie et la mort'. Cf. Bc45; Bd102.

Bc160 Goncourt, Edmond et Jules de, Refs in *Journal. Mémoires de la vie littéraire*, ed. Robert Ricatte, 22 vols, Monaco: Edns de l'Imprimerie nationale, 1956.
Useful insights into Z's personality, life-style, opinions and activities – although the comments are sometimes marked by malice and jealousy.

Bc161 González de Mendoza, J.M., 'L'influence de Z sur le roman mexicain', in Bb90, pp. 31-6.

Bc162 Gosse, Edmund, *Questions at Issue*, London: Heinemann, 1893, pp. 26-9.
In praise of Z's comprehensive treatment of 'the main interests of modern man'.

Bc163 Got, Olivier, 'Bordeaux vu par Z, 1870-1871', *Revue historique de Bordeaux et du Département de la Gironde*, XXII (1973), 103-20.
The atmosphere of the city where the National Assembly had been temporarily transferred as reflected in Z's correspondence; cf. EZ, *La République en marche, chroniques parlementaires*, ed. J. Kayser, Fasquelle, 1956.

Bc164 Gourmont, Remy de, 'Monsieur Z', in *Epilogues, réflexions sur la vie, 1re série, 1895-1898*, Mercure de France, 1903, pp. 30-4.

Bc165 ——, 'M. EZ', in *Epilogues, réflexions sur la vie, 3e série, 1902-1904*, Mercure de France, 1905, pp. 96-104.

Bc166 Grant, Elliott M., 'Z and the Sacré-Coeur', *FS*, XX (1966), 243-52.

Z's critical attitude to the controversial building of the Sacré-Coeur (as a votive offering following the *débâcle* of 1870) as reflected in newspaper articles and in *Paris*.

Bc167   Grant, Richard B., 'Un aspect négligé du style de Z', *CN*, 42 (1971), 13-21.
Suggests that judgments on Z's style would be much less unfavourable if, besides focusing on vocabulary, imagery, syntax and rhythm, his style were examined from the perspective of 'les grandes structures [i.e., the organizing themes] qui se retrouvent dans le microcosme du paragraphe'; examples are taken from *La Terre*, *L'Assommoir* and *Germinal*.

Bc168   Greaves, A.A., 'Trois figures de femme dans l'oeuvre de Z', *Revue de l'Université Laurentienne/Laurentian University Review* (Sudbury, Ontario), IV (Nov. 1971), 58-67.
Z's attitude towards women evolves from a preoccupation with 'la femme fatale' and 'la Béatrice' towards the gradual triumph of 'la collaboratrice'; this evolution mirrors Z's progress towards 'une conception optimiste du monde libéré de toute convention artificielle et soumis uniquement à l'amour humain'.

Bc169   Gross, David S., 'EZ as Political Reporter in 1871: What He Said and What He Had to Say', *Literature and History*, 7 (Spring 1978), 34-47.
A study of contradictions in Z's political attitudes with reference to his political journalism of 1871 and his treatment of political militancy in *Germinal* and *La Débâcle*. Cf. Bc170, 331; Bg27.

Bc170   Guedj, Aimé, 'Les révolutionnaires de Z', *CN*, 36 (1968), 123-37.
Excellent anatomy of 'les traits constitutifs d'un type unique' which reveals Z's deeply sceptical attitude towards the revolutionary figures he portrays and reinforces the Marxist charge that he is unable to envisage man as the agent of his own history. Cf. Bc169, 331; Bd130.

Bc171   Guichard, Léon, 'Les "Répétitions" de Z' and '*Les Rougon-Macquart* et *La Tétralogie*', in *La Musique et les lettres en France au temps du wagnérisme*, P.U.F., 1963, pp. 210-13.
'La puissance, le flot continu, la grandeur épique de certaines pages de Z font de lui un grand poète, mais sans que Wagner y soit pour rien'; cf. Bb16; Bc53, 54, 82, 251.

Bc172   Günther, Herbert, 'Z und Daudet. Ein ungleiches Freundespaar', in *Das unzerstörbare Erbe. Dichter der Weltliteratur. Fünfzehn*

Essays, Frankfurt am Main: Gesellschaft der Bibliophilen, 1973, pp. 79-85.

Bc173   Hamon, Philippe, 'A propos de l'impressionnisme de Z', *CN*, 34 (1967), 139-47.
A penetrating analysis of Z's narrative techniques and the evolution of his style in the light of Impressionism and post-Impressionism. Cf. Bc196, 297, 298; Bd365.

Bc174   ——, 'Z, romancier de la transparence', in Bb34, pp. 385-91.
'Nous assistons ... chez Z à un changement important de l'esthétique du Roman: ce n'est plus la multiplicité des sens possibles d'une oeuvre donnée qui fait la perfection de cette oeuvre, mais la multiplicité des procédés convergents qui foisonnent et qui concourent à l'élaboration d'un sens simple et non ambigu'; cf. Bc389.

Bc175   ——, Refs in 'Qu'est-ce qu'une description? ', *Poétique*, 12 (1972), 465-85.
An important discussion of the textual function of 'realist' description from a structuralist viewpoint: many examples are taken from Z. Cf.Bc177.

Bc176   ——, Review of Bb13, *CN*, 44 (1972), 228-33.
A stimulating critical assessment.

Bc177   ——, Refs in 'Un discours contraint', in Bb89, pp. 411-45.
Remarks on Z in the context of an essay towards a coherent structuralist theory of literary realism; complements Bc175.

Bc178   ——, Refs in 'Du savoir dans le texte', in Bb94, pp. 489-99.
Remarks on the textual manifestations of Z's desire to be 'scientific'.

Bc179   ——, Refs in 'Texte littéraire et métalangage', *Poétique*, 31 (1977), 261-84.

Bc180   ——, 'Note sur un dispositif naturaliste', in Bb84, pp. 101-1'8.
On the theme of the window; cf. Bc174, 389; Bd140.

Bc181   Hartley, K.H., 'Giovanni Verga and Z', *AUMLA*, 17 (1962), 70-6.

Bc182   Hatzfeld, Helmut A., Refs in *Literature through Art: A New Approach to French Literature*, New York: OUP, 1952.
Remarks on Z's descriptive impressionism.

Bc183   Heller, Adolphe B., ed., 'Six Letters from Champfleury to Z',

RR, LV (1964), 274-7.
Comments on the preface to *Thérèse Raquin* and on *La Fortune des Rougon* and *Madelaine Férat*.

Bc184 Hemmings, F.W.J., Refs in *The Russian Novel in France, 1884-1914*, London: OUP, 1950.

Bc185 ——, 'EZ et Louise Solari', *RHLF*, LX (1960), 60-1.
Cf. Bc158, 195.

Bc186 ——, 'Z pour ou contre Stendhal? ', *CN*, 19 (1961), 107-12.
Brings out Z's enduring affection for Stendhal; Z was both for and against Stendhal in that he, was incapable of understanding Stendhal's irony but much admired his depiction of love.

Bc187 ——, 'Stendhal relu par Z au temps de l'"Affaire" (documents inédits)', *Stendhal Club*, 16 (1962), 302-10.

Bc188 ——, 'EZ', *The Listener* (21.4.66), 574-80; repr. and tr. in *CN*, 33 (1967), 1-11.
Argues that Z's importance as an innovating novelist lies in the precedence of the social problems he treats over the drama of the individual, but points out that the impact of his best fiction depends less on its subject-matter than on the quality of imagination it reveals.

Bc189 ——, 'The Elaboration of Character in the *Ebauches* of Z's *Rougon-Macquart* Novels', *PMLA*, LXXXI (1966), 286-96.
A valuable examination of how Z's *Ebauches*, considered collectively, can be used as a source of information on his creative procedures, particularly in respect of the invention, modification and elaboration of his characters; stresses incidentally that the genesis of Z's novels rarely followed the same pattern.

Bc190 ——, 'Fire in Z's Fiction: Variations on an Elemental Theme', in Bb119, pp. 26-37.
An exploratory survey which traces only a few of the principal ramifications of a rich thematic complex. Fire is primarily a destructive element in Z; at the same time, fire may be both cathartic, burning away social impurities (the holocaust in *La Débâcle*, the destruction by fire of the factory L'Abîme in *Travail*) and a productive force ('la Côte-Verte' in *Germinal*, the noble smiths in 'Le Forgeron' and *L'Assommoir*, Morfain in *Travail*). Cf. Bd100, 102.

Bc191 ——, 'Intention et réalisation dans *Les Rougon-Macquart*', *CN*, 42 (1971), 93-108.

An illuminating examination of Z's initial plans for *Les Rougon-Macquart* (written in 1868-9) and their relationship to the completed fiction.

Bc192 ———, 'EZ devant l'Exposition Universelle de 1878', in Bb19, pp. 131-53.

Bc193 ———, 'Z, Novelist and Art-Critic' and 'Naturalism and Impressionism', in *Culture and Society in France 1848-1898. Dissidents and Philistines*, London: Batsford, 1971, pp. 194-8, 203-8.

Bc194 ———, ed., *The Age of Realism*, Harmondsworth: Penguin Books, 1974, pp. 179-94.

Bc195 Hoche, Jules, 'Le premier roman d'EZ', *La Revue illustrée*, IV (1887), 289-98.
Speculations on an unrequited adolescent passion for Louise Solari and its influence on Z's creative imagination. Cf. Bc158, 185.

Bc196 Hoefert, S., 'EZ dans la critique d'Otto Brahm', *CN*, 30 (1965), 145-52.
Brahm was the leading critic and theatrical director of the German Naturalist movement.

Bc197 Hoffman, Frederick J., 'From Document to Symbol: Z and American Naturalism', *Revue des langues vivantes*, XLII (1976), 203-12.

Bc198 Houston, John Porter, *Fictional Technique in France, 1802-1927. An Introduction*, Baton Rouge: Louisiana State U.P., 1972, pp. 84-91.
Superficial discussion of the narrative tone of *L'Assommoir* and the correlations of time and point of view, and poetic symbolism, in *Germinal*.

Bc199 Huret, Jules, Refs in *Enquête sur l'évolution littéraire*, Charpentier, 1891.
An account of numerous interviews with leading writers and critics on prevailing tendencies in literature; reflects the reaction against Naturalism.

Bc200 Huysmans, J.-K., 'EZ et *l'Assommoir*', *L'Actualité* (Brussels) (11, 18, 25 March and 1 April 1877); repr. in *En marge*, ed. Lucien Descaves, Lesage, 1927, pp. 7-40, and in *Oeuvres complètes*, Crès, 1928, vol.II, pp. 151-92 (pp. 160-6 repr. in George J. Becker, ed., *Documents of Modern Literary Realism*, Princeton U.P., 1963, pp. 232-5).

A general study of Z and a defence of Naturalism (despite the title).

Bc201 Ikor, Roger, 'Z et le lecteur d'aujourd'hui', in Bb34, pp. 348-56.
Reflections on Z's posthumous reputation and influence.

Bc202 ——, 'Z et nous', in Bb124, pp. 273-90.
Similar to preceding item.

Bc 203 James, Henry, 'EZ', *The Atlantic Monthly* (Boston), XCII (Aug. 1903), 193-210; repr. in *The House of Fiction*, ed. Leon Edel, London: Hart-Davis, 1957, pp. 220-49, and in George J. Becker, ed., *Documents of Modern Literary Realism* , Princeton U.P., 1963, pp. 506-34.
A perceptive and entertaining general assessment.

Bc204 Jean, Georges, 'Z ou la forge', in *Le Roman* (Coll. 'Peuple et culture'), Seuil, 1971, pp. 107-10.

Bc205 Jean, Raymond, 'L'exemple de Z', in *La Littérature et le réel. De Diderot au 'nouveau roman'*, Albin Michel, 1965, pp. 66-73.
A review of Bb50.

Bc206 Jeanne, René, 'EZ et le cinéma', in Bb90, pp. 204-13.
Cf. Bc152, 344; Bd191, 201, 326; Bf12.

Bc207 Jennings, Chantal, 'Z féministe? ', *CN*, 44 (1972), 172-87; 45 (1973), 1-22.
Despite Z's broadly sympathetic attitude towards female emancipation, his vision of the feminine ideal remained deeply paternalistic. Cf. Bb12.

Bc208 Joly, Bernard, 'Maupassant et Z', *CN*, 46 (1973), 205-26.

Bc209 Jones, Lawrence William, 'Steinbeck and Z: Theory and Practice of the Experimental Novel', *Steinbeck Quarterly*, IV (Fall 1971), 95-101.
Similarities between Z's theories and Steinbeck's fiction.

Bc210 Jones, Malcolm B., 'Translations of Z in the United States prior to 1900', *MLN*, LV (1940) 520-4.

Bc211 Jouhaux, Léon, 'Z et la classe ouvrière', in Bb90, pp. 158-62.
Z's popularity among the working classes and his influence, direct and indirect, on social reform.

Bc212 Jourdain, Francis, 'Z outragé et calomnié', in Bb90, pp. 131-9.

A sympathetic portrayal of Z's personality.

Bc213   Kahn, Maurice, 'Anatole France et Z', *La Grande Revue*, CXXI (July 1926), 40-66; repr. (same title) Lemarget, 1927.

Bc214   Kanes, Martin, 'Z, Flaubert et Tourgueniev: autour d'une correspondance', *CN*, 36 (1968), 173-81.

Bc215   Kantorowicz, Alfred, 'Heinrich Manns Essay über Z als Brennpunkt der Weltanschaulichen Beziehung zwischen Heinrich und Thomas Mann', *Neue Deutsche Literatur* (Berlin), III (May 1955), 96-109.
Cf. Bc216, 262, 263, 336.

Bc216   ——, 'Z — Essay — Betrachtungen eines Unpolitischen. Die paradigmatische Auseinandersetzung zwischen Heinrich und Thomas Mann', *Geschichte in Wissenschaft und Unterricht* (Stuttgart), XI (1960), 257-72.
Cf. Bc215, 262, 263, 336.

Bc217   Keins, Jean-Paul, 'Der historische Wahrheitsgehalt in den Romanen Zs', *Romanische Forschungen*, XLVI (1932), 361-96.

Bc218   Klotz, Volker, 'Die Stadt als Ausgabe. EZs Romanzyclus *Les Trois Villes* (1894-1898)', in *Die Erzählte Stadt. Ein Sujet als Herausforderung des Romans von Lesage bis Döblin*, Munich: Hanser, 1969, pp. 194-253.

Bc219   Knight, Everett, 'Z', in *A Theory of the Classical Novel*, London: Routledge & Kegan Paul, 1969, pp. 87-98.
A Marxist critique of the Naturalist aesthetic of impersonality.

Bc220   Kulczycka-Saloni, Janina, 'EZ en Pologne', *CN*, 32 (1966), 145-59.

Bc221   ——, 'La personnalité du romancier dans l'oeuvre de Z', in Bb34, pp. 83-91.

Bc222   ——, 'EZ vu par les Polonais', *Les Cahiers de Varsovie*, 2 (1973), 59-75.

Bc223   Laborde, Albert, *Trente-huit années près de Z. La Vie d'Alexandrine EZ*, Les Editeurs français réunis, 1963, *passim*.

Bc224   ——, 'Laissons parler Z', *CN*, 36 (1968), 161-72.

General remarks on Z's personality and his views on science, psychoanalysis and photography.

Bc225 ——, 'EZ à Médan: un entretien avec Albert Laborde', *CN*, 38 (1969), 146-68.
Detailed first-hand account of life in the Z household by the last survivor of Z's *familiers*;stresses Z's bourgeois tastes and his lack of interest in politics before the Dreyfus Affair.

Bc226 Lalo, Charles, 'Z, ou l'ascète du vice', in *L'Art et la vie: l'économie des passions*, Vrin, 1947, pp. 169-92.
A study of Z's personality: contrasts the *hardiesses* of his work with the discipline and asceticism of his private life.

Bc227 Lanoux, Armand, 'Z en proie aux tests', in Bb90, pp. 214-21.
An account of Bb111.

Bc228 Lanson, Gustave, 'Romanciers naturalistes: M. EZ', in *Histoire de la littérature française*, Hachette, 1895, pp. 1052-4; numerous re-edns.
Stresses the naïveté of Z's scientific pretensions and his limited powers of psychological analysis, but concedes that his fiction is redeemed by a powerful romantic imagination reminiscent of Hugo.

Bc229 Lapp, John C., 'Ludovic Halévy et EZ', *RDM* (15.7.1954), 323-7.

Bc230 ——. 'Z et l'article défini', *Le Français dans le monde*, XXVI (1958), 101-2.
Shows that the coupling of the indefinite article with an abstract noun is often used by Z as a form of personification which emphasizes the passivity of a character.

Bc231 ——, 'On Z's Habits of Revision', *MLN*, LXXIII (1958), 603-11.
Z's successive corrections of the page proofs of *Nana* and *Le Docteur Pascal*, and his corrections of the first edition of *La Joie de vivre*, show a concern for style for which he is rarely given credit.

Bc232 ——, 'The Watcher Betrayed and the Fatal Woman: Some Recurring Patterns in Z', *PMLA*, LXXIV (1959), 276-84.
Unconscious sexual obsessions of Z's are reflected throughout his fiction in recurrent scenes and situations: the passive lover or husband who witnesses his own displacement (Claude in *La Confession de Claude*, Guillaume in *Madeleine Férat*, Muffat in *Nana*); the Fatal Woman who embodies a perverse and malevolent sexuality (Madeleine Férat, Clorinde

Balbi in *Son Excellence Eugène Rougon*, Nana).

Bc233 ——, 'EZ et Ludovic Halévy: notes sur une correspondance', *CN*, 27 (1964), 91-100.

Bc234 ——, 'Z et le trait descriptif', *CN*, 42 (1971), 23-32.
Suggestive remarks on an aspect of Z's style.

Bc235 Larkin, Maurice, Refs in *Man and Society in Nineteenth-Century Realism: Determinism and Literature*, London: Macmillan, 1977 (esp. pp. 126-33).

Bc236 Le Blond, Maurice, 'Sur EZ', *MF*, CVI (1913), 5-19.

Bc237 ——, 'Naturalisme et naturisme', in *Essai sur le naturisme*, Mercure de France, 1896, pp. 113-27.

Bc238 Le Blond-Z, Jean-Claude, 'Gabriel Thyébaut, ami de Z', *CN*, 49 (1975), 15-29.

Bc239 ——. 'EZ et J.-K. Huysmans', *Bulletin de la Société Joris-Karl Huysmans*, XIV, 66 (1976), 12-21.

Bc240 Lecercle, Jean-Louis, 'De l'art impassible à la littérature militante: *Les Trois Villes* d'EZ, *La Pensée*, n.s., 46 (1953), 29-38.

Bc241 Lee, Vernon, 'The Moral Teaching of Z', *Contemporary Review* (London), LXIII (1893), 196-212.
Argues that the reader must face the 'horrors and indecencies' in Z's novels in order to gain 'the courage to face them in reality'.

Bc242 Leech, Clifford, 'Art and the Concept of Will', *Durham University Journal*, XLVIII (Dec. 1955), 1-7.
The example of Z is used to support the contention that 'within the determinist framework it is possible to have a rich and varied presentation of the human scene'.

Bc243 Lemaitre, Jules, 'EZ', in *Les Contemporains*, I, Lecène et Oudin, 1886, pp. 249-84.
A celebrated study by one of the first critics publicly to recognize Z's talent and to identify the epic quality of his work ('épopée pessimiste de l'animalité humaine').

Bc244 Lerner, Michael G., 'Edouard Rod et EZ, I: jusqu'en 1886', *CN*, 37 (1969), 41-58.

Bc245   ——, 'Edouard Rod and EZ, II: From *La Course à la mort* to Dreyfus', *NFS*, VIII (May 1969), 28-39.

Bc246   ——, 'Edouard Rod et EZ, III: l'Affaire Dreyfus et la mort de Z', *CN*, 40 (1970), 167-76.

Bc247   ——, 'Autour d'une conversation chez EZ', *Les Lettres romanes,* XXIV (1970), 265-72.
A comparison between two articles on Z by Edouard Rod and Paul Alexis.

Bc248   ——, 'Z et Taine: un manuscrit retrouvé', *CN*, 45 (1973), 97-100.

Bc249   Levin, Harry, 'Z', in *The Gates of Horn. A Study of Five French Realists*, New York: OUP, 1963, pp. 305-71.
Although it contains nothing fundamentally new, this general study of Z's work is suggestive, lively and learned.

Bc250   Lindsay, Jack, Refs in *Cézanne: His Life and Art*. London: Evelyn, Adams & Mackay, 1969.

Bc251   Lockspeiser, Edward. 'Z et le wagnérisme de son époque', in Bb34, pp. 324-8.
Cf. Bb16; Bc53, 54, 82, 171.

Bc252   Loos, Dorothy S., 'The Influence of EZ on the Five Major Naturalistic Novelists of Brazil', *Modern Language Journal*, XXXIX (1955), 3-8.

Bc253   López Jiménez, L., *El naturalismo y España: Valera frente a Z*, Madrid: Alhambra, 1977, *passim*.

Bc254   Lote, Georges, 'Z historien du Second Empire', *Revue des études napoléoniennes*, XIV (1918), 39-87.
A descriptive survey; praises the historical value of *Les Rougon-Macquart*, 'miroir véridique d'une époque'.

Bc255   Lüdeke, H., 'Z and the American Public', *English Studies* (Copenhagen), XXIII (1941), 129-42, 161-71.

Bc256   Lukács, Georg, 'The Z Centenary', in *Studies in European Realism*, tr. E. Bone, London: Hillway Publishing Co., 1950, pp. 85-
The most celebrated Marxist critique of Z's ideology. Magisterially dismisses Z's Naturalism as a debased and distorted form of Balzacian realism, arguing that his undialectical vision of society and his unparticipating approach to life are reflected in the cult of documentation, unselective

factual notation and non-typological characterization, while his lyrical stress on the mere outward scenery of life leads to a radical divorce between his characters and their social environments, thus reflecting a static and unprogressive world view.

Bc257 ——, Refs in *The Historical Novel*, London: Merlin Press, 1962; Harmondsworth: Penguin Books, 1969 (first pubd in Hungarian in 1947).

Bc258 ——, 'Narrate or Describe?', in *Writer and Critic and other essays*, ed. Arthur D. Kahn, London: Merlin Press, 1970, pp. 110-48.

Written in 1936. Includes a comparison between the exhaustive, virtuoso descriptions of the horse race and the theatre in *Nana* and similar scenes in Tolstoy's *Anna Karenina* and Balzac's *Illusions perdues* in order to bring out Z's static, contemplative approach to social reality: whereas in Tolstoy and Balzac we experience events which are inherently significant because of the participation of the characters in them and because of the general social significance that emerges from their impact on the characters' lives, in Z the scenes are only loosely related to the plot, they are described from the standpoint of an observer, and the descriptive details become important in themselves.

Bc259 Lützeler, Paul Michael, 'Erweiterter Naturalismus. Hermann Broch und EZ', *Zeitschrift für deutsche Philologie*, XCIII (1974), 214-38.

Bc260 Macchia, Giovanni, 'Z et la critique italienne', in Bb90, pp. 39-41.

Bc261 Magny, Claude-Edmonde, 'Z', in *Preuves*, 24 (1953), 30-45; repr. in *Littérature et critique*, Payot, 1971, pp. 362-82.

Bc262 Mann, Heinrich, 'Z', *Die Weissen Blätter* (Leipzig/Berlin), II, 11 (1915), 1312-82; repr. in *Macht und Mensch*, Munich: Kurt Wolff, 1919, pp. 35-131, and as Z, *Essay*, Leipzig: Insel, 1962.

Highly sympathetic; Mann felt a strong personal bond with Z, whom he admired for his integrity and vigour as a social critic. Cf. Bc215, 216, 336.

Bc263 Mann, Thomas, Refs in *Gesammelte Werke*, 13 vols, Frankfurt am Main: S. Fischer, 1974, esp. vol. XII (*Betrachtungen eines Unpolitischen*, first pubd in 1918).

Betrachtungen... contains Mann's lengthy response to the indirect criticism of his political conservatism embodied in Bc262. Cf. Bc215, 216.

Bc264 ——, 'Z et l'âge d'or', tr. Louise Servicen, in Bb90, pp. 11-12.

Describes Z as 'l'un des représentants les plus fortement marqués, les plus exemplaires, du XIXe siècle'; stresses symbolic and mythical expression in Z and his embodiment of a tradition – a lost 'golden age' – defined by a vigilant social consciousness.

Bc265　Mansuy, Michel, Refs in *Un Moderne: Paul Bourget. De l'enfance au 'Disciple'*, Les Belles Lettres, 1960, esp. pp. 224-49.

Bc266　Martino, Pierre, *Le Naturalisme français (1870-1895)*, Armand Colin, 1923; revised by R. Ricatte, 1965; 8th edn, ed. Ricatte, Colin (Coll. U2), 1969.

Bc267　Matthews, J.H., 'Z and the Marxists', *S*, XI (1957), 262-72.
A good summary of Marxist judgments on Z's theory and practice of the novel; fails to mention Barbusse (Bb8) and Aragon (Bc8).

Bc268　——, 'EZ and Gustave Le Bon', *MLN*, LXXIII (1958), 109-13.
Z's dramatic presentation of crowds in such novels as *Au Bonheur des Dames*, *Germinal* and *Lourdes* anticipated the principles formulated in Le Bon's *Psychologie des foules* (1895), giving proof of the novelist's genuine, instinctive comprehension of crowd psychology.

Bc269　——, '*Things* in the Naturalist Novel', *FS*, XIV (1960), 212-23.
An analysis of the description and role of 'things' in Z, far from indicating a concern with the mere accumulation of fortuitous detail, is an essential preliminary to an assessment of the Naturalists' conception of the universe and of man's place in it: things are used as symbolic keys to character, pointers to the compulsive presence of milieu, and hallucinatory projections of an environment to which the most rigorous determinism subjects man. Cf. Bd365.

Bc270　——, 'Z et les surréalistes', *CN*, 24-5 (1963), 99-107.
On aspects of Z's poetic vision and descriptive techniques which have affinities with surrealism.

Bc271　Maupassant, Guy de, 'EZ', in *Chroniques, études, correspondance de Guy de Maupassant*, ed. René Dumesnil, Gründ, 1938, pp. 76-8.

Bc272　Maurin, Mario, 'Z's Labyrinths', in Bb119, pp. 89-104.
A perceptive discussion of the theme of the labyrinth (mazes which lead to places often characterized by disorder and confusion) as a central motif of Z's imagination. The labyrinth has strong associations with eroticism, voyeurism, incest, and the past, and is fundamentally ambiguous in that the protection and fulfilment found within it are constantly interlinked with fear and death. Cf. Bc111, 114.

Bc273   Meakin, David, Refs in *Man & Work: Literature and Culture in Industrial Society*, London: Methuen, 1976 (esp. pp. 50-4, 119-22).
Some penetrating and well formulated observations on Z's cult of work, ethic of creativity and nostalgia for artisan values.

Bc274   Milner, George B., 'Z mis en relief par Cézanne', *Babel*, I, 1 (1940), 25-30.

Bc275   Mitterand, Henri, ed., 'Un projet inédit d'EZ en 1884-85: le roman des villes d'eaux', *CN*, 10 (1958), 401-23.

Bc276   ——, 'Un jeune homme de province à Paris: EZ de 1858 à 1861', *CN*, 11 (1958), 444-53.
Relates Z's disabused idealism to his development towards realism.

Bc277   ——, 'La jeunesse de Z et de Cézanne: observations nouvelles', *MF*, CCCXXXV (1959), 351-9.
On the circumstances of Cézanne's joining Z in Paris in 1861.

Bc278   ——, 'EZ à Marseille et à Bordeaux de septembre à décembre 1870. Lettres et documents inédits', *RSH*, 98-9 (1960), 257-87.
A presentation of, and commentary upon, fifteen letters Z wrote to his wife and mother jointly. Cf. Bc399.

Bc279   ——, 'Quelques aspects de la création littéraire dans l'oeuvre d'EZ', *CN*, 24-5 (1963), 9-20.
An important account of Z's creative method and the genesis of his novels.

Bc280   ——, 'Remarques d'introduction à l'étude des techniques de la composition et du style chez EZ', *CN*, 24-5 (1963), 79-81.
Some suggestive guidelines.

Bc281   ——, 'Le regard d'EZ', in Bb34, pp. 182-99; partially repr. in Ba12, pp. 73-8.
A masterly study (based mainly on the *dossiers* of *Les Rougon-Macquart*) of the richness and receptivity of Z's visual imagination and the role of pictorial observation ('la saisie sur le vif des êtres et des choses') in the genesis of his novels.

Bc282   ——, 'Histoire indiscrète d'une oeuvre', in Bb124, pp. 105-27.
A popular account of the genesis, structure, unity and poetic quality of *Les Rougon-Macquart*.

Bc283   ——, 'Les manuscrits perdus d'EZ', *CN*, 39 (1970), 83-90.

Bc284 ——, 'Français écrits et français littéraires', *Le Français dans le monde*, 69 (1969), 12-17.
Further remarks on Z's style.

Bc285 Monneret, Sophie, 'Z', in *Cézanne, Z... La fraternité du génie*, Denoël, 1978, pp. 35-68.

Bc286 Montreynaud, Florence, 'Les relations de Z et de Tourgueniev: documents inédits', *CN*, 43 (1972), 55-82.

Bc287 ——, 'Un journaliste russe chez Z, ou les étonnements de Boborykine', *CN*, 49 (1975), 83-101.
The impressions of a journalist who was the first to introduce Z's work to the Russian public.

Bc288 ——, 'Les relations de Z et de Tourgueniev (avec treize lettres inédites de Z à Tourgueniev)', *CN*, 52 (1978), 206-29.

Bc289 Moody, Joseph N., 'EZ: The Artist', 'EZ: The Propagandist', 'EZ: The Prophet', in *The Church as Enemy: Anticlericalism in Nineteenth Century French Literature*, Washington: Corpus Books, 1968, pp. 155-222.

Bc290 ——, 'French Anticlericalism: Image and Reality', *Catholic Historical Review*, LVI (1971), 630-48 (pp. 643-8).
Compares the anticlericalism of Z's later works with that of Michelet.

Bc291 Moore, George, 'My Impressions of Z', in *Impressions and Opinions*, London: Werner Laurie, 1913, pp. 66-84; repr. as 'A Visit to Médan', in *Confessions of a Young Man*, London: Heinemann, 1926, pp. 268-77.

Bc292 Morgan, O.R., 'Léon Hennique et EZ', *CN*, 30 (1965), 139-44.

Bc293 Muller-Campbell, Denise E., 'Le thème de la culpabilité masculine dans l'oeuvre d'EZ', *CN*, 46 (1973), 165-81.
Z's treatment of man/woman relationships reveals his firm belief in masculine responsibility towards women.

Bc294 Naudin-Patriat, Françoise, 'Les classes laborieuses face à l'institution du mariage dans les *Rougon-Macquart*', *CN*, 50 (1976), 191-201.

Bc295 Neuschäfer, Hans-Jörg, 'EZ und die Mythen des Industriezeiters', in *Populärromane im 19. Jahrhundert. Von Dumas bis Z*, Munich:

Fink, 1976, pp. 163-97.
A lively sociological study.

Bc296   Newton, Joy, 'EZ impressionniste', *CN*, 33 (1967), 39-52; 34 (1967), 124-38.
A well documented account of affinities in theory, subject-matter and technique between Z and the Impressionists. Cf. Bc173, 297, 298; Bd365.

Bc297   ——, 'Z et l'expressionnisme: le point de vue hallucinatoire', *CN*, 41 (1971), 1-14.
Centres on affinities between Z and Van Gogh (use of light, sun and colour, 'animisme', reflection of mood in landscapes); in both cases a highly personal vision is imposed on external reality. Cf. Bc173, 296, 298; Bd365.

Bc298   ——, 'EZ and the French Impressionist Novel', *L'Esprit créateur*, XIII (Winter 1973), 320-8.
Shows how the exchange of ideas and themes between Z and the Impressionists ('a kind of osmosis') worked in the best way possible for both sides; cf. Bc173, 296, 297; Bd365.

Bc299   ——, and Monique Fol, 'Z et Rodin', *CN*, 51 (1977), 177-85.

Bc300   ——, 'L'esthétique de Z et de Rodin, "le Z de la sculpture"', *CN*, 53 (1979), 75-80.

Bc301   Nicholas, Brian, 'Z', in John Cruickshank, ed., *French Literature and its Background*, V: *The Late Nineteenth Century*, London: OUP, 1969, pp. 154-72.

Bc302   Niess, Robert J., 'EZ and Edmond de Goncourt', *American Society of Legion of Honor Magazine*, XLI (1970), 85-105.

Bc303   ——, 'Le thème de la violence dans les *Rougon-Macquart*', *CN*, 42 (1971), 131-9.
Cf. Bc402.

Bc304   ——, 'EZ: la femme au travail', *CN*, 50 (1976), 40-58.
'... c'est [Z] qui a dépeint assez de travailleuses pour établir un canon artistique et fonder un type littéraire'.

Bc305   ——, 'Conspiracy, Complicity and Guilty Knowledge in Z's Rougon-Macquart Series', in Grant E. Kaiser, ed., *Fiction, Form, Experience/Fiction, forme, expérience*, Montreal: Edns France-Québec, 1976, pp. 67-82.
On Z's heavy reliance on plots, conspiracies and complicities throughout

the series to evoke the social climate of the Second Empire.

————: see also Bc54.

Bc306   Noiray, Jacques, 'La machine et les structures de l'imaginaire dans les romans de Z', *Annales du Centre de recherches sur l'Amérique anglophone* (Univ. de Bordeaux III), III (1974), 96-1
Cf. Bb13 (pp. 76-124); Bc125.

Bc307   Osborne, John, 'Ibsen, Z and the Development of the Naturalistic Movement in Germany', *Arcadia*, II (1967), 196-205.

Bc308   Paraf, Pierre, 'EZ et Henri Barbusse', *CN*, 46 (1973), 139-45.
Outlines the affinities between the two writers.

Bc309   Pascal, Roy, 'EZ – use and abuse', in *The Dual Voice: Free Indirect Speech and its Functioning in the Nineteenth-Century European Novel*, Manchester U.P.; Totowa, New Jersey: Rowman & Littlefield, 1977, pp. 112-22.
Examples are taken from *Germinal* and *La Terre*.

Bc310   Payot, Roger, 'EZ, ou la ressemblance contrariée', *CN*, 44 (1972), 158-71.
On the thematic and structural unity of *Les Rougon-Macquart*.

Bc311   Pelletier, Jacques, 'Lukács, lecteur de Z', *CN*, 41 (1971), 58-74.
A detailed exposition and brief critique of Bc256.

Bc312   ————, 'Z évangéliste', *CN*, 48 (1974), 205-14.
A general account of *Les Quatre Evangiles*.

Bc313   ————, 'Z, la femme et le Christ: la mise en scène d'un fantasme', *Protée*, IV (Autumn 1975), 53-64.
A predominantly psychoanalytic reading of Z's treatment of the Church and the figure of the priest (with particular ref. to *La Conquête de Plassans* and *Vérité*).

Bc314   Peter, René, 'Z et l'Académie', *MF*, CCXCVI (1940), 568-82.

Bc315   Petrey, Sandy, 'Obscenity and Revolution', *Diacritics*, III (Fall 1973), 22-6.
A provocative review-article on Bb13 which carries further Borie's view that the connection in the nineteenth-century bourgeois psyche between the body and the lower classes, and the structuring of social and mental categories so as to conceal both the bourgeoisie's physical nature and the

workers' humanity, means that Z's obscenity, by forcing the reader to recognize that the human condition is a universal, had a powerfully subversive effect on the ideological justification for the capitalist hierarchy; Z's novels, by their power to shatter bourgeois thought, are revolutionary in impact and thus do not deserve customary Marxist reprobation.

Bc316   ——, 'Sociocriticism and *Les Rougon-Macquart*', *L'Esprit créateur*, XIV (Fall 1974), 219-35.

Stimulating discussion, with reference to Z, of methodological issues raised by recent French essays in *sociocritique* (cf. Bc175, 177; Bd193-6), which addresses itself to the social vision implicit in a text's linguistic structure rather than to the social entity a text describes; while commending the fruitfulness of sociocritics' intrinsic approach to social fiction, Petrey challenges their classification of Z as a petty-bourgeois reactionary by proposing modifications to the theoretical presuppositions which tend to justify this view: the failure of sociocriticism to explore the ways in which literary techniques interact with as well as transcend social and historical reference is responsible for its misrepresentation of the textual function of social discourse. Cf. Bd89.

Bc317   Pia, Pascal, 'EZ', in *Romanciers, poètes et essayistes du XIXe siècle*, Denoël, 1971, pp. 426-41.

Reviews of EZ, *La République en marche, chroniques parlementaires*, ed. J. Kayser, Fasquelle, 1956, Bb50 and Bb51.

Bc318   Picon, Gaëtan, 'Le "réalisme" d'EZ: du "tel quel" à l'oeuvre-objet', *CN*, 22 (1962), 235-40.

Interesting observations on authorial presence, point of view, epic inflation and artistic autonomy.

Bc319   Pillu, Pierre, 'Vallès et Z', in Bb34, pp. 328-35.

Bc320   Pomilio, Mario, 'EZ', in *Dal naturalismo al verismo*, Naples: Liguori, 1963, pp. 26-42.

Bc321   Powers, Lyall, 'Henry James and Z's *Roman expérimental*', *University of Toronto Quarterly*, XXX (1960), 16-30.

The influence on James of Z's theories on heredity and milieu.

Bc322   Randal, Georges, 'EZ et l'Académie française', *Aesculape*, n.s., XXXIV (1953), 18-23.

Bc323   Rébérioux, Madeleine, 'Z et la critique littéraire française socialiste et anarchiste, 1894-1902', in Bb34, pp. 7-16.

Bc324   Reizov, B., 'Affrontements de traditions littéraires dans *Les Frères Karamazov*', *RLC*, XLVI (1972), 219-41 (pp. 228-41).
Z's influence on Dostoevsky.

Bc325   Remak, Henry H., Refs in 'The German Reception of French Realism', *PMLA*, LXIX (1954), 410-31.
Continues the work of Root (Bb101) by tracing Z's reputation in Germany since 1893.

Bc326   Reuillard, Gabriel, 'L'amitié littéraire d'EZ pour Gustave Flaubert', *Les Amis de Flaubert*, 4 (1953), 11-20.

Bc327   Rewald, John, ed., *Paul Cézanne: correspondance*, Grasset, 1937, *passim*; English tr.: London: Cassirer, 1941.

Bc328   ——, *Cézanne, sa vie, son oeuvre, son amitié pour Z*, Albin Michel, 1939; English tr.: *Paul Cézanne: A Biography*, New York: Simon & Schuster, 1948; London: Spring, n.d.

Bc329   ——, Refs in *The History of Impressionism*, New York: Museum of Modern Art, 1946.

Bc330   Ripoll, Roger, 'Fascination et fatalité: le regard dans l'oeuvre de Z', *CN*, 32 (1966), 104-16; partially repr. in Ba12, pp. 96-105.
Analysis of variations on the theme of 'le regard' and its dramatic function: recurring theme (nudity, 'le spectacle défendu', children as witnesses, the voyeur, triangular situations) reveal personal 'obsessions' concerning sexuality and death. Cf. Bc232.

Bc331   ——, 'Z et les Communards', in Bb34, pp. 16-26.
Z's presentation of the Commune as destructive anarchism and collective folly in *La Débâcle* and in his journalistic account of it in *Le Sémaphore de Marseille* corresponds to his negative portrayal of revolutionary figures in *Le Ventre de Paris*, 'Jacques Damour' (a short story) and *Germinal*. Cf. Bb80 (pp. 139-52); Bc169, 170; Bd130; Bg27.

Bc332   ——, 'La vie aixoise dans les *Rougon-Macquart*', *CN*, 43 (1972), 39-54.

Bc333   Robert, Guy, ed., 'Une polémique entre Z et le *Mémorial d'Aix* en 1868', *Arts et livres* (Marseilles), 6 (1946), 5-23.

Bc334   ——, 'Le document au service de la création poétique', in Bb90, pp. 179-82; repr. in Ba12, pp. 78-82.

Bc335   Robert, Louis de, 'Alphonse Daudet et EZ', in *De Loti à Proust. Souvenirs et confidences*, Flammarion, 1928, pp. 121-49.

Bc336   Roberts, David, '*Wirklichkeit oder Gedicht*: The Z Essay of Heinrich Mann', *FMLS*, VI (1970), 243-54.
Cf. Bc215, 216, 262, 382.

Bc337   Rod, Edouard, 'M. EZ', in *Les Idées morales du temps présent*, Perrin, 1891, pp. 73-98.
Perceptive general study; discusses the tension between Z *moraliste* and Z *savant*.

Bc338   ——, 'The Place of EZ in Literature', *Contemporary Review* (London), LXXXII (1902), 617-31.
A favourable estimate; some overlap with preceding item.

Bc339   Rossat-Mignod, Suzanne, 'L'évolution des théories de Z', in Bb33, pp. 148-54.
A strikingly indulgent Marxist view.

Bc340   Rosselli, Ferdinando, *Una polemica letteraria in Spagna: il Romanzo Naturalista*, Pisa: Istituto di Letteratura Spagnola e Ispano-Americana, 1963, *passim*.
Z's influence in Spain.

Bc341   Roudomino, M., 'EZ et les lecteurs soviétiques', in Bb33, pp. 173-6.
Z's popularity in Russia.

Bc342   Roy, Claude, 'Le génie de l'amour sublimé', in Bb124, pp. 153-70.
Argues that 'ce chaste est un écrivain érotique non seulement intense et brûlant, mais subtil et juste', and that sexual fulfilment with Jeanne Rozerot spelt artistic mediocrity.

Bc343   Rubenach, Jane, ed., 'Une correspondance inédite entre EZ et Jules Clarétie', *CN*, 51 (1977), 149-76.

Bc344   Sadoul, Georges, 'Z et le cinéma français (1900-1920)', in Bb33, pp. 158-70.
Cf. Bc153, 206; Bd191, 201, 326; Bf12.

Bc345   Salvan, Albert J., 'Lafcadio Hearn's Views on the Realism of Z', *PMLA*, LXVII (1952), 1163-7.
Hearn was one of the first translators of Z in the United States, but felt no moral, aesthetic or spiritual sympathy for him.

Bc346   ——, 'Z's American Correspondents', *American Society of Legion of Honor Magazine*, XXXI (1960), 153-63.

Bc347   ——, 'Z critique de son oeuvre dans sa correspondance', in Bb34, pp. 336-41.

Bc348   Sanders, J., 'EZ: le transplanté et l'arbre', in Grant E. Kaiser, ed., *Fiction, Form, Experience/Fiction, forme, expérience*, Montreal: Edns France-Québec, 1976, pp. 53-66.
On the richness of tree symbolism throughout Z's work.

Bc349   Schmidt, Günter, 'Die Rezeption von Vererbungsauffassungen durch EZ', in *Die literarische Rezeption des Darwinismus. Das Problem der Vererbung bei EZ und im Drama des deutschen Naturalismus*, Berlin: Akademie-Verlag, 1974, pp. 80-131.

Bc350   Schober, Rita, 'Z', in *Skizzen zur Literaturtheorie*, Berlin: Deutscher Verlag der Wissenschaften, 1956, pp. 62-5.
Argues that Z's world-view was fundamentally *petit-bourgeois*.

Bc351   ——, 'Observations sur quelques procédés stylistiques de Z', *CN*, 28 (1964), 149-61.
A study of lexical and image patterns in the light of Z's Naturalist theories.

Bc352   ——, 'L'actualité de Z en R.D.A.', in Bb34, pp. 222-31.
A well documented account of the evolution of Z's reputation in Germany.

Bc353   ——, 'Zu einigen sprachlichen Problemen literarischer Übersetzung dargelegt an Hand der Titel-Übersetzung von Zs *Rougon-Macquart*', *Beiträge zur Romanischen Philologie*, XV (1977), 117-46.

Bc354   ——, 'Für oder wider Z: zum Verhältnis von Rezeption, Kritik und Bewertung', *Weimarer Beiträge: Zeitschrift für Literaturwissenschaft, Aesthetik und Kulturtheorie*, XXIII, 3 (1977), 5-43.
A review of reactions to Z in the German-speaking world from the 1870s to the present day.

Bc355   Schor, Naomi, 'Introduction', in Bb119, pp. 5-7.
Suggests that the renaissance in Z scholarship since 1952 results directly from the general renewal of French criticism during that period and that the generally thematic approach adopted by many of the contributors to Bb119 reflects a current and very rewarding trend in Z criticism.

Bc356 ——, 'Mother's Day: Z's Women', *Diacritics*, V (Winter 1975),
11-17.
A searching review-article on Bb62 and Bd229.

Bc357 ——, 'Le sourire du sphinx: Z et l'énigme de la féminité', *Roman-*
tisme, 13-14 (1976), 183-95.
The problematics of femininity in Z illuminated through patterns of pre-
Oedipal sexuality in *La Joie de vivre*, *Nana* and *Une Page d'amour*.

Bc358 Schor, Ira N., 'The Novel in History: Lukács and Z', *Clio*, II
(1972), 19-41.
Argues that the stultifying effects of scientism on Z have been exaggerated,
particularly by Lukács, who unnecessarily denigrated *Germinal* as a product
of Z's bourgeois origins. Although disagreeing with Lukács's assessment of
Z as a defeatist observer, contends that Lukács, with his insistence that
ideology is a question of form no less than of content, can be an important
source for a 'new marxist criticism'; the usefulness of Lukács's formalist
methods is demonstrated by the application of his theory of the novel to
Germinal (especially), *La Débâcle* and *Vérité* (briefly). Cf. Bc256, 257, 258.

Bc359 Schulz-Buschaus, Ulrich, 'Z, Adorno und die Geschichte der
nichtkanonisierten Literatur. Anmerkungen zu H.-J. Neuschafers
Populärromane im 19. Jahrhundert', *Archiv für das Studium*
der Neueren Sprachen, 214 (1977), 376-88.
A review-article on Bc295.

Bc360 Sigaux, Gilbert, '*Les Rougon-Macquart* en 1962', *CN*, 22 (1962),
241-8.
A review of Z's reputation.

Bc361 Simon, Pierre-Henri, 'Un des derniers disciples de Rousseau',
CN, 38 (1969), 105-14.

Bc362 Stein, Barbara, 'Physiologische Merkmale bei Klassenbezeich-
nungen im Wortschatz EZs', *Wissenschaftliche Zeitschrift der*
Martin-Luther-Universität Halle-Wittenberg. Gesellschafts- und
Sprachenwissenschaftliche Reihe, XIX (1970), 189-207.
A painstaking lexical and thematic study which attempts to show how Z's
political *parti pris* emerges from the vocabulary he uses to represent social
classes.

Bc363 Steinmetz, Jean-Luc, 'Interscriptions (Mallarmé-Z)', in Bb94,
pp. 597-617.
Examines the ways in which the art criticism of Mallarmé and Z, Z's

estimate of Mallarmé's work (in particular, his criticism that Mallarmé is excessively preoccupied with form), and (especially) Mallarmé's perceptive responses to Z's fiction (reflected mainly in Bb74) provide insights into the aesthetic attitudes of both writers.

Bc364   Suffel, Jacques, 'L'odorat d'EZ', *Aesculape*, n.s., XXXIII (1952), 204-7.

Bc365   Tancock, Leonard W., 'On Translating Z', in *Balzac and the Nineteenth Century. Studies in French Literature presented to Herbert J. Hunt*, ed. D.G. Charlton, J. Gaudon and A.R. Pugh, Leicester U.P., 1972, pp. 377-89.
Reflections by Z's most distinguished translator.

Bc366   Ternois, René, 'Z et Verga', *CN*, 14 (1960), 541-54.

Bc367   ——, 'Le stoïcisme d'EZ', *CN*, 23 (1963), 289-98.
Z's positivist ideology seen in the context of the idealist reaction against positivism (Bourget, Brunetière, etc.); *Le Docteur Pascal* seen as Z's 'testament philosophique'.

Bc368   Thibaudet, Albert, 'Réflexions sur la littérature. Le groupe de Médan', *NRF*, XV (1920), 923-33.

Bc369   ——, 'Réflexions sur Z', *NRF*, XLV (1935), 906-12; repr. in *Réflexions sur la littérature*, II, Gallimard, 1940, pp. 295-300.

Bc370   ——, *Histoire de la littérature française de 1789 à nos jours*, Stock, 1936, pp. 371-5.

Bc371   Thody, Philip, 'The Politics of the Family Novel: Is Conservatism Inevitable? ', *Mosaic*, III (1969), 87-101.
Contrasts the radical attack on the capitalist system embodied in *Les Rougon-Macquart* (not really a family novel in the sense that Z's characters do not deliberately try to model themselves on a family pattern) with the merely intermittent social protest contained in the work of Galsworthy, Thomas Mann, Martin du Gard and Duhamel, and suggests that the family novel may be, through its very nature, basically conservative. Cf. Bc415.

Bc372   Thomson, Clive R., 'Discours social et discours idéologique: l'étude génétique des romans de Z', *CN*, 50 (1976), 202-12.
A useful discussion of methodological principles.

Bc373   ——, 'Une correspondance inédite (première partie): vingt-sept lettres de Marius Roux à EZ (1864-1869)', in Bb95, pp. 335-70.

Bc374 Tindall, William York, 'Troughs of Zolaism', in *Forces in Modern British Literature, 1885-1946*, New York: Knopf, 1947, pp. 145-84.
Z's influence.

Bc375 Tison-Braun, Micheline, 'Z et l'apostolat humanitaire', in *La Crise de l'humanisme. Le Conflit de l'individu et de la société dans la littérature française moderne*, I: *1890-1914*, Nizet, 1958, pp. 292-313.
The social idealism of Z's later works mirrors the 'renouvellement d'espoir qui marque, au début du siècle, la pensée libérale'.

Bc376 Tolstoy, Leo, 'Z et Dumas: le non-agir', in *Z, Dumas, Guy de Maupassant*, tr. E. Halpérine-Kaminsky, Léon Chailley, 1896, pp. 47-91.
A commentary on Z's speech, 'A la jeunesse' (1893); advocates Christian ideals rather than Z's materialist faith in science and social engineering.

Bc377 Trilling, Lionel, 'In Defense of Z', in *A Gathering of Fugitives*, London: Secker & Warburg, 1957, pp. 12-19.
A review of Bb118 (Wilson's stress on Z's 'black poetry' and on his fascinated horror of sex is fully endorsed) and of a new translation of *Pot-Bouille* (seen as a masterpiece of comic morality).

Bc378 Turnell, Martin, 'Z et l'Angleterre', in Bb90, pp. 13-16.
Brief remarks on Z's reputation and influence.

Bc379 ——, 'Z', in *The Art of French Fiction*, London: Hamish Hamilton, 1959, pp. 91-194.
A general presentation of *Les Rougon-Macquart* which attempts to define the cycle's unity of vision in terms of the mythic themes of Fertility and Genesis (cf. Bb99 and Bc387); five novels, considered the most representative, receive separate treatment: *Le Ventre de Paris*, *L'Assommoir*, *Nana*, *Germinal*, *La Terre*; concludes with a section on Z's style.

Bc380 Vallès, Jules, 'Notes d'un absent', *Le Voltaire* (22.12.1878 and 26.12.1878); repr. in Jules Vallès, *Littérature et révolution. Recueil de textes littéraires*, ed. Roger Bellet, Les Editeurs français réunis, 1969, pp. 367-74, 375-81.
A defence of Z's article 'Les Romanciers contemporains' (pubd in *Vestnik Evropy* in Sept. 1878 and incorporated into *Les Romanciers naturalistes* [1881]).

Bc381 ——, 'Dickens et Z', *Le Voltaire* (11.2.1880); repr. in Jules Vallès,

Littérature et révolution. Recueil de textes littéraires, ed. Roger Bellet, Les Editeurs français réunis, 1969, pp. 391-7.
On a meeting with Z in 1863 or 1864 (when the latter worked for Hachette).

Bc382 Vanhelleputte, Michel, 'L'essai de Heinrich Mann sur EZ', *Revue des langues vivantes*, XXIX (1963), 510-20.
Cf. Bc215, 216, 262, 336.

Bc383 Vinchon, Jean, 'Z dîne avec les Goncourt', *Aesculape*, n.s., XXXIV (1953), 1-7.
Reflections of Z's personality in Bc160.

Bc384 ——, 'Un psychiatre relit Z', in Bb90, pp. 222-7.
Argues that, through the writing of *La Confession de Claude*, *La Joie de vivre* and *L'Oeuvre*, Z was able progressively to liberate himself from his neuropathy: 'ces livres ont eu pour lui la même valeur qu'une psychanalyse efficace'.

Bc385 Wais, K., Refs in 'Zur Auswirkung des französischen naturalistischen Romans auf Deutschland', in *An den Grenzen der Nationalliteraturen. Vergleichende Aufsätze*, Berlin: Walter de Gruyter & Co., 1958, pp. 215-36.

Bc386 Walcutt, Charles Child, 'Z: The Fountainhead of Naturalistic Theory and Practice', in *American Literary Naturalism. A Divided Stream*, Minneapolis: Univ. of Minnesota Press, 1956, pp. 30-44.

Bc387 Walker, Philip D., 'Prophetic Myths in Z', *PMLA*, LXXIV (1959), 444-52; partially repr. in Ba12, pp. 156-62.
Influential analysis of parallels in *La Faute de l'abbé Mouret*, *Germinal* and *La Débâcle* with Hebraic, Greco-Roman and Celtic myths of death and resurrection, world destruction and renewal; argues that Z's mythopoeism expresses an essentially modern vision and portrays symbolically the birth of the contemporary world.

Bc388 ——, '*The Octopus* and Z: A New Look', *S*, XXI (1967), 155-65.
Shows the differences between Z and Frank Norris 'even in those areas in which they most closely resemble each other'.

Bc389 ——, 'The Mirror, the Window, and the Eye in Z's Fiction', in Bb119, pp. 52-67.
Argues that the multiplicity of mirrors, windows, eyes and viewpoint characters in Z's fiction represent the principal means whereby he achieves his ascent from an objective view of the world to an all-embracing religious and philo-

sophical perception of human reality. Cf. Bc174.

Bc390   ——, 'The Survival of Romantic Pantheism in Z's Religious
Thought', *S*, XXIII (1969), 354-65.
Argues that Z was at heart a pantheist deeply rooted in the romantic tradition, and stresses that, far from being an atheist or even a consistent ag-
nostic, Z was a spiritually restless, deeply religious man hovering eternally
between the two poles of doubt and faith.

Bc391   ——, 'Z et la lutte avec l'Ange', *CN*, 42 (1971), 72-92.
The Biblical story of Jacob and the angel was seen by Z as a symbol of his
own life, which is characterized as 'une lutte incessante, pénible, pour
passer du doute à la certitude, de l'ignorance à une vision rédemptrice du
monde'.

Bc392   ——, 'Z, Myth, and the Birth of the Modern World', *S*, XXV
(1971), 204-20.
More evidence that however much Z identified himself with the modern
scientific mentality, 'the mythopoeic mind, which he associated with the
doomed world of the past, not only survived in him but took on in his
imagination a brilliant new vitality'; his choice of myths (reflecting the
themes of world destruction and renewal) reveals his status as a transitional figure, a 'mythopoet of the modernization process'.

Bc393   ——, 'Z: Poet of an Age of Transition', in Bb32, pp. 3-10.
The themes of transition, progress, world destruction and renewal are
central, unifying themes of Z's fiction: 'Z is a kind of modern Ovid...
concerned with the metamorphosis of an entire society'.

Bc394   ——, 'Z's Hellenism', in *The Persistent Voice. Essays on Hellenism in French Literature since the 18th Century in Honor of
Professor Henry M. Peyre*, ed. Walter G. Langlois, New York
U.P.; Geneva: Droz, 1971, pp. 61-77.
A painstaking examination of sources which shows that Z's roots extend
much more deeply into the Hellenist tradition than most critics had pre-
viously suspected. Cf. Bf69.

Bc395   Walter, Rodolphe, 'Z et ses amis à Bennecourt (1886)', *CN*, 17
(1961), 19-35.
The first of several meticulously documented accounts of Z's stays at Bennecourt, on the Seine, and his close contacts there with Impressionist painters;
these articles shed light on the autobiographical and factual basis of *L'Oeuvre*;
cf. Bd352, 353.

Bc396   ——, 'EZ et Paul Cézanne à Bennecourt, en 1886', *Le Mantois*

(Bulletin de la Société 'Les Amis du Mantois'), 12 (1961), 1-40.

Bc397 ——, 'EZ et Claude Monet ', *CN*, 26 (1964), 51-61.

Bc398 ——, 'EZ à Bennecourt en 1868: les vacances d'un chroniqueur', *CN*, 37 (1969), 29-40.

Bc399 ——, 'Z et la Commune: un exil volontaire', *CN*, 43 (1973), 25-37
A careful reconstruction of Z's movements after the outbreak of the Commune; complements Bc278.

Bc400 Weinberg, Henry, 'Le style et la thématique de l'intimité chez Z', in Bb84, pp. 149-61.
A psychocritical analysis of 'l'obsession du trou' in some early texts (1868-72

Bc401 Weiske, Fritz, Zs Stellung zum Katholizismus nach seinen Romanen *Lourdes, Rome, Paris*', *Germanisch-romanische Monatsschrift* (Heidelberg), XXIV (1936), 127-44.

Bc402 Wenger, Jared, 'The Art of the Flashlight: Violent Technique in *Les Rougon-Macquart*', *PMLA*, LVII (1942), 1137-59.
Forms of melodramatic violence in Z as reflected in plot-formulas, character-types and characteristic episodes. Cf. Bc303.

Bc403 ——, 'Character-Types of Scott, Balzac, Dickens, Z', *PMLA*, LXII (1947), 213-32.

Bc404 White, Lucien, 'Z's Commercialism', *FR*, XXX (1956-7), 20-4.

Bc405 ——, 'EZ's Romanticism Judged by His Contemporaries and by Himself', *MLQ*, XVIII (1957), 206-10.

Bc406 ——, 'Moral Aspects of Z's Naturalism Judged by His Contemporaries and by Himself', *MLQ*, XXIII (1962), 360-72.

Bc407 Wilson, Nelly, 'Propos de Z sur le sionisme (1900)', *CN*, 40 (1970) 151-66
Z's reactions to Jewish nationalism, especially as reflected in *Vérité* and his notes for *Justice*.

Bc408 Wolfzettel, Friedrich, 'Die strukturelle Bedeutung des Fremden-Motivs in den *Rougon-Macquart* von Z', *Germanisch-romanische Monatsschrift* (Heidelberg), n.s., XXI (1971), 28-42.
Argues that the figure of the outsider in Z represents the desire to change confronted with a hostile, pre-rational world governed by immutable,

cyclical laws; the frustration of the outsider's attempts to penetrate this world, reflected in the themes of sexual failure, sterility and temporal enclosure, is not only grounded in Z's private preoccupations but represents his awareness of individual alienation in mass society.

Bc409 ——, Refs in 'Funktionswandel Eines Epischen Motivs: Der Blick auf Paris', *Romanistische Zeitschrift für Literaturgeschichte* (Heidelberg), I (1977), 353-76 (pp. 365-8).
Z's treatment of the city; cf. Bc78, 89.

Bc410 Wurmser, André, 'Les marxistes, Balzac et Z', *CN*, 28 (1964), 137-48; repr. in *Conseils de révision*, Gallimard, 1972, pp. 176-93.
Conciliatory Marxist view which, although criticizing Z's positivist aesthetic, stresses the similarities between Balzac and Z (contrast Bc255), Z's exemplary stand over Dreyfus, and his 'progressive' social outlook.

Bc411 ——, 'Le monde du travail', in Bb124, pp. 209-30; repr. as '*Travail* et le monde du travail' in *Conseils de révision*, Gallimard, 1972, pp. 222-50.

Bc412 Zéraffa, Michel, Refs in *Roman et société*, P.U.F., 1971 (esp. pp. 137-8).

Bc413 Zévaès, Alexandre, 'EZ et Jules Guesde', *Commune*, 42 (1937), 689-95.

Bc414 ——, 'Une correspondance entre EZ et Jules Vallès', *Commune*, 53 (1938), 552-63.
A series of letters (written in 1876-9) which reflect the sympathy between the two writers and Z's attempts to help Vallès in his literary career.

Bc415 Zucker, A.E., 'The Genealogical Novel: A New Genre', *PMLA*, XLIII (1928), 551-60.
Compares Z with Samuel Butler and discusses the influence of Z's idea of a genealogical novel, affording a panorama of several generations, on Thomas Mann, John Galsworthy, American fiction of the 1920s and Maxim Gorky. Cf. Bc371.

Bd   Fiction

L'Argent (1881)

Alas, Leopoldo: see Bd4.

Bd1   Bédé, Jean-Albert, 'The Secret Sources of the Bourse According to Balzac and Z', *American Society of Legion of Honor Magazine*, XXX (1959), 165-77.
L'Argent compared with *La Maison Nucingen*.

Bd2   Bouvier, Jean, '*L'Argent*: roman et réalité', in Bb34, pp. 54-64.
On the documentary value of *L'Argent*.

Bd3   ——, 'Le monde des affaires', in Bb124, pp. 171-91.
On the relationship between historical reality and literary creation; stresses Z's ambiguous attitude towards capitalism as an economic system.

Bd4   Clarín [Leopoldo Alas], 'Z y su última novela. *L'Argent*', in *Ensayos y revistas, 1888-1892*, Madrid: Manuel Fernández y Lasanta, 1892, pp. 57-79.
An admiring review.

Bd5   Cohen, Gaston, '*L'Argent*', in Bb33, pp. 107-11.
An amusing demonstration that *L'Argent* may be read as a virtual vindication of capitalism.

Bd6   Grant, Richard B., 'The Jewish Question in Z's *L'Argent*', *PMLA*, LXX (1955), 955-67.

Bd7   ——, 'The Problem of Z's Character Creation in *L'Argent*', *Kentucky Foreign Language Quarterly*, VIII (1961), 58-65.
The general artificiality and an occasional inconsistency in the characterization are explained by the fact that 'the characters were developed as [Z] composed his novel, and they came into being, not for themselves, but to support the ideas or narrative'.

Bd8   Joachimescu-Graur, Théodosia, 'Préface à une édition roumaine de *L'Argent*', in Bb33, pp. 187-200.

Bd9   Lafargue, Paul, '*L'Argent* de Z', in *Critiques littéraires*, Edns sociales internationales, 1936, pp. 173-211 (written in 1891-2).
A critical view of the novel from a socialist standpoint.

Bd10   Suwala, Halina, 'A propos de quelques sources de *l'Argent*', *CN*,

16 (1960), 651-4.

Bd11 ——, 'Le krach de l'Union Générale dans le roman français avant *l'Argent* de Z', *CN*, 27 (1964), 80-90.

Bd12 Verhaeren, Emile, 'Z: *L'Argent*', in *Impressions*, 2e série, Mercure de France, 1927, pp. 195-202.
On Z's lyrical evocations of the city.

Bd13 Wurmser, André, '*L'Argent* et le monde de l'argent', in *Conseils de révision*, Gallimard, 1972, pp. 194-221.
A predictable critique of Z's failure to locate the reasons for the catastrophe he describes in the capitalist system itself.

See also Bb41, 63, 79.

L'Assommoir (1877)

Bd14 Albérès, R.-M., 'Que révèle *L'Assommoir* en 1967? ', *Revue de Paris*, LXXIV (Feb. 1967), 51-9.
Stresses the artistic unity of *L'Assommoir*, seen as 'une forme de création qui se montre somme toute aussi rigoureuse qu'une tragédie classique'. Cf. Bd16.

Bd15 Baguley, David, 'Event and Structure: The Plot of *L'Assommoir*', *PMLA*, XC (1975), 823-33.
Thorough analysis of the rigorous formal unity of *L'Assommoir* as revealed by the organic development of its plot. The novel's internal organization reveals a system of interrelated features deriving from a scheme of three controlling structural oppositions reflected throughout the novel in character, action and description: work/idleness, cleanliness/filth, abstention/indulgence. The development of the plot, marked by a symmetrical pattern of measured gradation, is the process by which Gervaise and Coupeau progressively abandon the positive values of this scheme and submit to the opposite tendencies. This carefully integrated rising and falling action contrasts with Z's theoretical pronouncements in favour of the developing tendency in novel writing to disrupt the logical progression of plot.

Bd16 ——, 'Rite et tragédie dans *l'Assommoir*', *CN*, 52 (1978), 80-96.
A distinguished reading of the novel in terms of the formal and thematic characteristics of tragic literature. Cf. Bd14.

Bd17 Becker, Colette, 'La condition ouvrière dans *l'Assommoir*: un inéluctable enlisement', *CN*, 52 (1978), 42-57.

Z's pessimistic vision of the workers' condition is reflected in the predominance of images and motifs which reinforce a sense of inevitable *enlisement*.

Bd18   Block, Haskell M., *Naturalistic Triptych: The Fictive and the Real in Z, Mann, and Dreiser*, New York: Random House, 1970 (see esp. 'Z's *L'Assommoir*', pp. 16-31).
Intelligent exploration of *L'Assommoir* (together with Mann's *Buddenbrooks* and Dreiser's *An American Tragedy*) in order to clarify the ideological and aesthetic meanings of the term 'naturalism'; properly stresses the need to evaluate naturalistic fiction, not according to the expressed theories of the novelists, but in relation to the fiction itself, and affirms that 'naturalism and artistic creation are fully compatible'.

Bd19   Boutan, Pierre, 'Z, Hugo et *L'Assommoir*: littérature et politique', in *Recherches en sciences des textes. Hommage à Pierre Albouy*, Presses universitaires de Grenoble, 1977, pp. 55-73.
Aesthetic/political correlations in contemporary press reactions to the novel.

Bd20   Chambron, Jacqueline, 'Réalisme et épopée chez Z: de *L'Assommoir* à *Germinal*', *La Pensée*, n.s., 44 (1952), 122-34.
The 'epic' *Germinal* gives a deeper insight into working-class problems and class conflict than the 'lyrical' *L'Assommoir*.

Bd21   Cogny, Pierre, 'Z et *Le Sublime* de Denis Poulot', in Bb19, pp. 113-29.
Cf. Bd32.

Bd22   Cressot, Marcel, 'La langue de *l'Assommoir*', *Le Français moderne*, VIII (1940), 207-18.

Bd23   Davoine, Jean-Pierre, 'Le pronom, sujet disjoint dans le style indirect libre de Z', *Le Français moderne*. XXXVIII (1970), 447-51.

Bd24   De Sanctis, Francesco, 'Z e *L'Assommoir*', in *Saggi Critici*, ed. Luigi Russo, 3 vols, Bari: Laterza, 1952, vol. III, pp. 277-99; repr. in *Il Manifesto del realismo*, ed. Rino Dal Sasso, Rome: Editori Riuniti, 1972, pp. 91-116.
A lecture given in 1879; cf. Bc11, 38, 107.

Bd25   Gaillard, Françoise, 'A chacun sa vérité', *CN*, 52 (1978), 17-26.
Argues that the Naturalist aesthetic of objectivity explains the power of *L'Assommoir* as an attack on bourgeois ideology.

Bd26   Gaillard, Jeanne, 'Réalités ouvrières et réalisme dans *l'Assommoir*', *CN*, 52 (1978), 31-41.

On the value of the novel for the social historian.

Bd27 Gregor, Ian, and Brian Nicholas, 'The Novel as Social Document: *L'Assommoir*', in *The Moral and the Story*, London: Faber, 1962, pp. 63-97.

Intelligent exploration of the novel from the perspective of moral consciousness. Argues that the novel's characterization (which makes Gervaise representative of the working-class society of Paris), structure (portraying Gervaise as acting within a larger pattern of social pressures which underline the relentlessly destructive forces of environment and the radical undermining of the individual will) and narrative technique (in which the narrative viewpoint becomes blurred, anonymous and relative) reflect an aesthetic unconcerned with the raising of moral issues or the recognition of moral distinctions; concludes that such an aesthetic, by insidiously demoting its characters from the status of individual moral beings to that of helpless sociological specimens, has 'strictly limited potentialities'. Cf. Bd41.

Bd28 Grobe, Edwin P., 'Narrative Technique in *L'Assommoir*', in Bb32, pp. 56-66.

Analysis of the novel's 'dominant narrative modes in terms of their relative conformity to either bourgeois or working-class language habits'; stresses the range, virtuosity and unobtrusiveness of Z's narrative technique; and argues that 'whatever doctrinaire assumptions initially generated their creation, the novels of Z in general, and *L'Assommoir* in particular, affect us deeply because the use of a multiple narrative style attenuates the theoretical severity of Z's literary doctrine and communicates his overriding humanitarian concern for his subjects'.

Bd29 Harneit, Rudolf, 'Eine ideale Liebe in einem naturalistischen Roman. Zur Gestalt des Goujet in Zs *L'Assommoir*', in *Aufsätze zur Themen- und Motivgeschichte. Festschrift für Hellmuth Petriconi*, Hamburg: Cram, De Gruyter in Kommission, 1965, pp. 151-70.

Etsablishes parallels with Flaubert's *L'Education sentimentale*.

Bd30 Kédros, André, 'Lettre à M. Z à propos de *L'Assommoir*', in Bb33, pp. 65-71.

A forceful restatement of the old charge that Z's lack of clear *engagement* in *L'Assommoir* renders the book ineffective as a work of social criticism, for it is overloaded with odious secondary characters, portrays the *déchéance* of the protagonists in a fatalistic light, implies that they lack any political consciousness, and presents ascension to the bourgeoisie as the only avenue of escape open to them: '... il faut avouer, maître, que votre roman ne suscite chez le bourgeois ni la mauvaise conscience, ni la peur, au contraire: il affermit et légitime chez lui son mépris du peuple et son arrogance'.

Bd31 Léonard, Martine, '*L'Assommoir*, langage de l'"autre"', *Etudes françaises*, X (1974), 41-60.
A detailed analysis of the novel's syntax which shows how the written language merges with the spoken.

Bd32 Leroy, Maxime, 'Le Prolétariat au milieu du XIXe siècle décrit par Denis Poulot dans *Le Sublime* et par EZ dans *L'Assommoir*', in *Histoires des idées sociales en France*, III, Gallimard, 1954, pp. 246-57.
Cf. Bd21.

Bd33 Livanský, Karel, 'EZ — auteur des premiers romans sur le prolétariat français', *Philologica Pragensia* (Prague), XVI (1973), 171-5.
A banal restatement of the standard Marxist judgment that Z's portrayal of the proletariat in *L'Assommoir*, although artistically powerful, is distorted and limited by his positivist outlook.

Bd34 Michot-Dietrick, Hela, 'Blindness to "Goodness": The Critics' Chauvinism? An Analysis of Four Novels by Z and the Goncourts', *Modern Fiction Studies*, XXI (1975), 215-22.
Argues that, as most critics have contended, 'uterine frenzy' is to blame for much of the misery suffered by Gervaise Macquart, Nana and the protagonists of *Germinie Lacerteux* and *La Fille Elisa*, but that it is merely a manifestation of their naïve generosity ('bonté'), which itself reflects their desire for love; the fact that critics have overlooked the social significance of their 'bonté' signifies bourgeois chauvinism rather than male chauvinism, for 'the ability to perform the act of generosity is denied the poor by society through the simple fact that being good exhausts their limited energy and their meagre resources'.

Bd35 Newton, Joy, and Basil Jackson, 'Z et l'expression du temps: horlogerie obsessionnelle dans *L'Assommoir*', *NFS*, XVII (May 1978), 52-7.
Analysis of the temporal images which reflect 'l'écoulement d'une vie sans espoir de restitution'.

Bd36 Niess, Robert J., 'Remarks on the *style indirect libre* in *L'Assommoir*', *NCFS*, III (1974-5), 124-35.

Bd37 Ochman, Daniela, 'Le lexique du milieu populaire dans *L'Assommoir* d'EZ, *Acta Universitatis Wratislaviensis* (Romanica Wratislaviensia, Wroclaw), 265 (1975), 91-116.

Bd38 Petrey, Sandy, 'Goujet as God and Worker in *L'Assommoir*', *French Forum*, I (1976), 239-50.

Far from representing a solution to working-class problems by the cultivation of the bourgeois virtues of work, thrift and abstinence, Goujet typifies 'false consciousness', i.e., uncritical acceptance of an ideology which does nothing to relieve his actual socio-economic circumstances.

Bd39 ——, 'Le discours du travail dans *l'Assommoir*', *CN*, 52 (1978), 58-67.
On the ideological implications of the style chosen to describe the characters at work.

Bd40 Petrovska, Marija, 'Les sons et le silence dans les romans de Z (*L'Assommoir, Germinal, La Bête humaine*)', *Romance Notes*, XIV (Winter 1972), 289-98.
On Z's skilful use of sounds and silence either to prepare the proper atmosphere for a dramatic event or to bring to life his personified objects.

Bd41 Place, David, 'Z and the Working Class: The Meaning of *L'Assommoir*', *FS*, XXVIII (1974), 39-49.
The characterization of Gervaise (a representative figure conditioned by her social situation and whose experience is thus not amenable to moralistic solutions) contrasts with that of Goujet (an idealized moral type); the ambiguity of the novel arises from this conflict between moralistic and sociological attitudes to the social problems portrayed. Cf. Bd27.

Bd42 Pritchett, V.S., *Books in General*, London: Chatto & Windus, 1953, pp. 116-22.

Bd43 Richman, Michèle, 'After the Festival', *MLN*, XCIII (1978), 750-5.
A review of Bb31.

Bd44 Schor, Naomi, 'Sainte-Anne: capitale du délire', *CN*, 52 (1978), 97-108.
Argues that *L'Assommoir* is 'un méta-roman, le seul roman sur l'écriture que Z ait jamais écrit'.

Bd45 Vissière, Jean-Louis, 'L'Art de la phrase dans *L'Assommoir*', *CN*, II (1958), 455-64.
Stresses Z's varied use of *style indirect libre* to reflect the patterns of popular speech; illustrates his familiarity with *l'écriture artiste* and how *L'Assommoir* is a most carefully written novel despite its exploitation of a demotic idiom.

Bd46 Walker, Philip, '*L'Assommoir* et la pensée religieuse de Z', *CN*, 52 (1978), 68-79.
The values embodied in *L'Assommoir* reflect aspirations which may be termed

religious; cf. Bd224.

Bd47   Weinberg, Henry H., 'Les "Femmes du peuple" de Francis: une nouvelle source de *l'Assommoir*? ', *CN*, 39 (1970), 61-9.

See also Bb4, 9, 26, 31, 41, 63, 76, 79; Bc198, 200, 379, 411; Bd18; Be21, 31, 32.

Au Bonheur des Dames (1883)

Bd48   Bouvier-Ajam, Maurice, 'Z et les magasins de nouveautés (*Au Bonheur des Dames*)', in Bb34, pp. 47-54.

Bd49   Candille, Marcel, 'De la réalité au roman. *Au Bon Marché* de M. et Mme Boucicaut, et *Au Bonheur des Dames* d'EZ', *Revue de l'Assistance publique à Paris*, IV (1953), 75-91.

Bd50   Dupuy, Aimé, 'Les grands magasins et leur "histoire littéraire"', *L'Information historique*, XX (1958), 106-12.

Bd51   Niess, Robert J., 'Z's *Au Bonheur des Dames*: The Making of a Symbol', in *Symbolism and Modern Literature. Studies in Honor of Wallace Fowlie*, ed. Marcel Tétel, Durham, N.C.: Duke U.P., 1978, pp. 130-50.
Good analysis of rhetorical devices employed by Z to support the powerful central symbol of the store.

Bd52   Ten Brink, Jan, '*Au Bonheur des Dames*', in *Nieuwe Romans*, Haarlem: Tjeenk Willink, 1883, pp. 113-42.
Important from a literary-historical viewpoint; cf. Bb108; Bd310.

See also Bb63; Bc268.

La Bête humaine (1890)

Bd53   Baroli, Marc, 'Le Train au centre d'un roman avec Z', in *Le Train dans la littérature française*, Edns N.M., 1963, pp. 207-66.
A systematic analysis of the genesis of the novel, its documentary value, its narrative structure and epic qualities, the symbolic function of La Lison, contemporary critical reactions, and the novel's influence.

Bd54   Bonnefis, Philippe, 'L'inénarrable même', *CN*, 48 (1974), 125-40.

A penetrating analysis of Z's narrative art in *La Bête humaine*.

Bd55 Deleuze, Gilles, 'Z et la fêlure', in *Logique du sens*, Edns de minuit, 1969, pp. 373-86; Union générale d'édns (série 10/18), 1973, pp. 424-36; partially repr. in Ba12, pp. 44-9.
A subtle discussion of the hereditary 'fêlure' of Z's characters as expressive of the death-instinct; this fatality is worked out in the destiny of Jacques Lantier and is figured in the epic symbol of the train.

Bd56 Dentan, Michel, 'A propos d'un chapitre de *La Bête humaine*', *Etudes de lettres*, X (July-Sept. 1977), 31-42.
An explication of the second chapter.

Bd57 Duchet, Claude, '*La Fille abandonnée* et *La Bête humaine*: éléments de titrologie romanesque', *Littérature*, 12 (1973), 49-73.

Bd58 Feldman, A. Bronson, 'Z and the Riddle of Sadism', in H.M. Ruiten-beck, ed., *Psychoanalysis and Literature*, New York: Dutton, 1964, pp. 272-81.
A psychoanalytic explication that anticipates some of the analyses of Borie (Bb13).

Bd59 Franchi, Danièle, and Roger Ripoll, 'Douceur et intimité dans *la Bête humaine*', *CN*, 51 (1977), 80-90.
Perceptive analysis of 'douceur et intimité' in the structural and thematic elaboration of the novel.

Bd60 Grant, Elliott M., 'L'Affaire Poinsot-Jud, Mérimée, et Z', *CN*, 23 (1963), 313-5.
A well-publicized crime in 1860 was echoed in Mérimée's *La Chambre bleue* and the murder of Grandmorin in *La Bête humaine*.

Bd61 Lombroso, Cesare, '*La Bête humaine* et l'anthropologie criminelle', *Revue des revues*, IV, 23 (June 1892), 260-4.

Bd62 Matoré, Georges, 'A propos du vocabulaire des couleurs', *Annales de l'Université de Paris*, XXVIII (1958), 137-50 (p. 143).
On the use of colour in *La Bête humaine* and *Germinal.*

Bd63 Matthews, J.H., 'The Railway in Z's *La Bête humaine*', *S*, XIV (1960), 53-9.
La Bête humaine is not a documentary study subjoined to a novel about homicidal insanity, for Z exploits the dramatic and symbolic possibilities of the railway setting to intensify the hallucinatory atmosphere of his main theme.

Bd64 Scott, J.W., 'Réalisme et réalité dans *La Bête humaine*: Z et les chemins de fer', *RHLF*, LXIII (1963), 635-43.
A careful demonstration of 'le caractère ... nonchalant de la documentation ferroviaire du romancier'.

See also Bb26, 58, 60; Bc9, 125; Bd40, 342; Bf4.

La Confession de Claude (1865)

Bd65 Cressot, Marcel, 'Z et Michelet. Essai sur la genèse de deux romans de jeunesse: *La Confession de Claude, Madeleine Férat*', *RHLF*, XXXV (1928), 382-9.

Bd66 Greaves, A.A., 'Religion et réalité dans l'oeuvre de Z', in Bb34, pp. 122-9.
Good analysis of the psychology of Z's protagonist.

Bd67 Lapp, John C., 'The Critical Reception of Z's *Confession de Claude*', *MLN*, LXVIII (1953), 457-62.

Bd68 Weinstein, Sophie R., 'The Genesis of Z's *La Confession de Claude*', *MLN*, LIII (1938), 196-8.

See also Bb50, 61; Bc232, 384.

La Conquête de Plassans (1874)

Bd69 Dubois, Jacques, '*Madame Gervaisais* et *La Conquête de Plassans*: deux destinées parallèles, deux compositions qui s'opposent', *CN*, 24-5 (1963), 83-9.
Shrewd comparison of the treatment of erotico-religious hysteria in Z and the Goncourts, showing the greater imaginative force and structural unity of *La Conquête de Plassans*, and its greater development of the erotic theme.

Bd70 Dupuy, Aimé, Refs in 'Esquisse d'un tableau du roman politique français', *Revue française de science politique*, IV (1954), 484-513.
Remarks on *La Conquête de Plassans* and *Son Excellence Eugène Rougon*.

Bd71 Schor, Naomi, 'Le délire d'interprétation: naturalisme et paranoïa', in Bb84, pp. 237-55.
An exploration of 'la folie textuelle'.

Bd72   Slater, Judith, 'Echoes of Balzac's Provincial Scenes in *La Con-quête de Plassans*', *Modern Languages*, LX (1979), 156-61.

See also Bc18, 313, 332.

La Curée (1872)

Bd73   Alcorn, Clayton, '*La Curée*: les deux Renée Saccard', *CN*, 51 (1977), 49-55.
Contrasts the stereotype envisaged in the preparatory dossier with the complex individual described in the novel.

Bd74   Auriant, L., 'EZ et les deux Houssaye', *MF*, CCXCVII (1940), 555-69.
Arsène and Henri Houssaye were used as models for Saccard and Maxime.

Bd75   Bourneuf, Roland, 'Retour et variation des formes dans *La Curée*', *RHLF*, LXIX (1969), 993-1008.
The structural and thematic unity of the novel is created by recurrent motifs within a particular scene (examples are taken from Chapter IV), the repetition of similar scenes (especially the episodes in the hothouse), and the omnipresence of key images (flowers, fire, water). Cf. Bd79.

Bd76   Citron, Suzanne, '*La Curée* dans une classe de première', in Bb34, pp. 235-40.

Bd77   Dezalay, Auguste, 'La "nouvelle Phèdre" de Z ou les mésaventures d'un personnage tragique', *TLLS*, IX (1971), 121-34.
On Z's exploitation of the theme of Phèdre. Cf. Bd91.

Bd78   Durand, Gilbert, 'Les mythes et symboles de l'intimité et le XIXe siècle: contribution à la mythocritique', in *Intime, intimité, intimisme*, Univ. de Lille III: Edns universitaires, 1976, pp. 81-98 (pp. 89-96).
On the 'décor mythique' of *La Curée*; cf. Bd265.

Bd79   Godenne, Janine, 'Le tableau chez Z: une forme, un microcosme', *CN*, 40 (1970), 135-43.
The example of *La Curée* is taken to illustrate the important structural uses of the 'tableau' in Z. Cf. Bd75.

Bd80   Grant, Elliott M., 'The Composition of *La Curée*', *RR*, XLV (1954), 29-44.

Bd81 Joly, Bernard, 'Le chaud et le froid dans *la Curée*', *CN*, 51 (1977), 56-79.
A sensitive thematic analysis.

Bd82 Lethbridge, Robert, 'Du nouveau sur la genèse de *La Curée*', *CN*, 45 (1973), 23-30.

Bd83 ——, 'La préparation de *la Curée*: mise au point d'une chronologie', *CN*, 51 (1977), 37-48.

Bd84 ——, 'Une "conspiration du silence"? — Autour de la publication de *la Curée*', *Les Lettres romanes*, XXXI (1977), 203-19.

Bd85 ——, 'Z: Decadence and Autobiography in the Genesis of a Fictional Character', *NFS*, XVII (May 1978), 39-51.
Traces the elaboration of Maxime as a figure accommodating a number of different concerns, fictional, polemical and symbolic.

Bd86 ——, 'Z and Taine: New Light on a Literary Relationship', *Romance Notes*, XIX (Fall 1978), 29-32.
On a possible borrowing from Taine's *Graindorge*.

Bd87 Nelson, Brian, 'Speculation and Dissipation: A Reading of Z's *La Curée*', *Essays in French Literature*, 14 (1977), 1-33.
Illustrates the ways in which Z articulates a satirical vision of Second Empire society through his deployment of a highly expressive metaphoric language, relates his descriptive impressionism to his basic themes, and suggests that the thematic centre of the novel, viewed as a coherent totality, lies in Z's vision of the appalling waste of human energies.

Bd88 ——, 'Z's Metaphoric Language: A Paragraph from *La Curée*', *Modern Languages*, LIX (1978), 61-4.

Bd89 Petrey, Sandy, 'Stylistics and Society in *La Curée*', *MLN*, LXXXIX (1974), 626-40.
A stimulating exploration of the ways in which *La Curée*, both as a social novel and as a psychological study, is a unified textual representation of social reification: the thematic axis of Z's exposure of financial and political corruption functions as the stylistic and symbolic axis for his narration of Renée's incest and psychological destruction; the alienated and dehumanized quality of existence in a society which worships money is apparent in the images, mythic allusions, descriptive terminology and rhetorical devices which organize the language recounting Renée's incestuous affair. Textual analysis of *La Curée* thus compels a sort of 'sociostylistics'. Cf. Bc316.

Bd90   Ripoll, Roger, 'L'histoire du Second Empire dans *la Curée*', *Revue d'histoire moderne et contemporaine*, XXI (1974), 46-57.

Bd91   Via, Sara, 'Une Phèdre décadente chez les naturalistes', *RSH*, 153 (1974), 29-38.
Positing the idea that Decadentism is 'une évolution particulière' rather than a reaction against Naturalism, analyses *La Curée* in conjunction with Alexis's *Madame Meuriot* and argues that Z's treatment of 'la femme fatale' (Renée) and the 'éphèbe vicieux' (Maxime) is in the decadent idiom. Cf. Bd77.

Bd92   Wolfzettel, Friedrich, 'Vertikale Symbolik in EZs *La Curée*', *Germanisch-romanische Monatsschrift* (Heidelberg), n.s., XIX (1969), 435-43.
Sensitive analysis of the metaphoric patterns that translate the downward spiral of Renée's life and, by extension, the Second Empire itself.

See also Bb63, 79; Bc80, 316, 409; Be32.

La Débâcle (1892)

Bd93   Bouthoul, Gaston, 'Actualité de *La Débâcle*', in Bb90, pp. 163-70.

Bd94   De Vogüé, Eugène-Melchior, '*La Débâcle* d'EZ', *RDM*, CXII (1892), 443-58.
Compares Z with Tolstoy.

Bd95   Manceau, Henri, 'Sur les chemins ardennais de *La Débâcle*', in Bb33, pp. 136-48.
An account of Z's visit to the Ardennes in preparation for *La Débâcle*.

Bd96   Nicoletti, Gianni, 'Z e i militari', in *Saggi e idee di letteratura francese*, Bari: Adriatica, 1965, pp. 259-74.

Bd97   Petriconi, Hellmuth, '*La Débâcle*', in *Das Reich des Untergangs*, Hamburg: Hoffmann & Campe, 1958, pp. 37-66.

Bd98   Raitt, A.W., 'EZ (1840-1902): From *La Débâcle*', in *Life and Letters in France*, III: *The Nineteenth Century*, London: Nelson, 1965, pp. 127-34.
Discusses Z's diagnosis of the Franco-Prussian disaster and stresses the extent of the ramifications of 1870 in French attitudes and ideas.

Bd99   Rhodes, S.A., 'The Source of Z's Medical References in *La Débâcle*',

MLN, XLV (1930), 109-11.

See also Bb102; Bc117, 169, 331, 358, 387, 409.

Le Docteur Pascal (1893)

Bd100   Bachelard, Gaston, *La Psychanalyse du feu*, Gallimard, 1938, pp. 189-92.
On the extraordinary death by spontaneous combustion of Antoine Macquart: 'Un tel récit ... donne à penser que Z a construit son image de la science avec ses rêveries les plus naïves et que ses théories de l'hérédité obéissent à la simple intuition d'un passé qui s'inscrit dans une matière sous une forme sans doute aussi pauvrement substantialiste, aussi platement réaliste que la *concentration* d'un alcool dans une chair, du feu dans un coeur en fièvre.' Cf. Bc190; Bd102.

Bd101   Baguley, David, 'Du naturalisme au mythe: l'alchimie du docteur Pascal', *CN*, 48 (1974), 141-63.
Argues that the novel is less concerned with the celebration of science than with the mythical themes of fecundity and renewal, articulated principally through the relationship between Pascal and Clotilde.

Bd102   Butor, Michel, 'EZ, romancier expérimental, et la flamme bleue', *Critique*, 239 (1967), 407-37; repr. in *Répertoire IV*, Edns de minuit, 1974, pp. 259-91; shortened version: 'Au feu des pages', *CN*, 36 (1967), 101-13 (repr. in English in Bb119, pp. 9-25, and partially repr. in Ba12, pp. 89-96).
Attempts to bring out the richness of Z's physiological imagination with reference to fluids: blood, associated with the Rougons, is equated with the themes of common hereditary guilt and usurpation; alcohol, which characterizes the Macquarts, partially neutralizes the effects of usurpative blood; milk and water — life-giving fluids — symbolize fertility and rejuvenation. Cf. Bc45, 159, 190; Bd100.

Bd103   D'Annunzio, Gabriele, 'La morale di EZ (*Le Docteur Pascal*)', *La Tribuna*, 3, 10 and 15.7.1893; repr. in *Pagine disperse. Cronache mondane, letteratura, arte*, ed. Alighiero Castelli, Rome: Bernardo Lux, 1913, pp. 555-72.
A negative assessment.

Bd104   Malinas, Yves, 'Z, précurseur de la pensée scientifique du XXe siècle', *CN*, 40 (1970), 108-20.

A cogent defence of Z's scientific pretensions as reflected in *Le Docteur Pascal*: 'à travers des contresens qui furent ceux de son siècle, la pensée de Z sait dépasser les faits incertains et les théories éphémères pour atteindre à une philosophie de la connaissance qui est très proche de celle qui nous est familière.'

Bd105   Schober, Rita, 'Der Doktor Pascal oder vom Sinn des Lebens', *Beiträge zur romanischen Philologie*, XII (1973), 317-43.

Bd106   ——, '*Le Docteur Pascal* ou le sens de la vie', *CN*, 53 (1979), 53-74.
Translation of Bd105.

Bd107   Toubin, Catherine, and Yves Malinas, 'Les clés et les portes (essai sur la symbolique du *Docteur Pascal*)', *CN*, 41 (1971), 15-22.
A study in sexual symbolism.

Bd108   Wolfzettel, Friedrich, '*Le Docteur Pascal* und seine Bedeutung für den Rougon-Macquart-Zyklus Zs', *Die Neueren Sprachen*, LXXI (n.s. XI) (1972), 148-60.

See also Bc34, 349, 367; Bf56.

La Faute de l'abbé Mouret (1875)

Bd109   Brown, Calvin S., 'Parallel Incidents in EZ and Tomasi di Lampedusa', *Comparative Literature*, XV (1963), 193-202.

Bd110   Brown, Donald F., 'Two Naturalistic Versions of Genesis: Z and Pardo Bazán', *MLN*, LII (1937), 243-8.
Compares *La Faute de l'abbé Mouret* with *La madre naturaleza*.

Bd111   Grant, Richard B., 'Confusion of Meaning in Z's *La Faute de l'abbé Mouret*', *S*, XIII (1959), 284-9.
Z's adaptation of the Genesis myth led him to introduce the idea of sin, whereas the union of Serge and Albine was not intended to be seen as shameful.

Bd112   Greaves, A.A., 'A Comparison of the Treatment of Some Decadent Themes in *La Faute de l'abbé Mouret* and *La Joie de vivre*', in *Proceedings: Pacific Northwest Conference on Foreign Languages* (1966), pp. 98-107.

Bd113   ——, 'Mysticisme et pessimisme dans *La Faute de l'abbé Mouret*', *CN*, 36 (1968), 148-55.
The basic themes of the novel interpreted in the light of the philosophy of Schopenhauer.

Bd114   Hemmings, F.W.J., 'The Secret Sources of *La Faute de l'abbé Mouret*', *FS*, XIII (1959), 226-39.
A careful examination of the literary sources of the novel — in particular, the idyll of Silvère and Miette in the wild garden echoes that of Marius and Cosette in Hugo's *Les Misérables*.

Bd115   ——, 'EZ et la religion. A propos de *La Faute de l'abbé Mouret*', in Bb34, pp. 129-35.
Far from being an anti-religious pamphlet, *La Faute de l'abbé Mouret* is an allegorical dramatization of the conflict between the two religions of paganism and Christianity.

Bd116   Minogue, Valerie, 'Z's Mythology: That Forbidden Tree', *FMLS*, XIV (1978), 217-30.
A searching study of the mythological implications of Z's neo-pagan re-writing of the Fall of Man.

Bd117   Musumeci, Antonino, 'Tasso, Z and the Vicissitudes of Pastoralism', *NCFS*, IV (1975-6), 344-60.
Uses Tasso's *Aminta* as a frame of reference by which to measure Z's (ultimately inadequate) adoption of pastoralism as a *vision du monde* in *La Faute de l'abbé Mouret*.

Bd118   Newton, Joy, and Monique Fol, 'Z et le clair-obscur', *CN*, 47 (1974), 98-105.
Z's symbolic use of *le clair-obscur* in *La Faute de l'abbé Mouret* and *Germinal*.

Bd119   Ormerod, Beverley, 'Z's Enclosed Gardens', *Essays in French Literature*, II (1974), 35-46.
Argues that the idyll is closely linked with the realistic sections of the novel through the recurring image of an enclosed garden.

Bd120   Pasco, Allan H., 'Literary History and Quinet in the Meaning of *La Faute de l'abbé Mouret*', *FMLS*, XIV (1978), 208-16.
An interpretation of the novel in the light of Quinet's and others' interest in the evolution of man from savagery to civilization.

Bd121   Ripoll, Roger, 'Le symbolisme végétal dans *La Faute de l'abbé*

Mouret: réminiscences et obsessions', *CN*, 31 (1966), 11-22.
A searching analysis of the mythic dimension of *La Faute de l'abbé Mouret* (the thematic centre of the novel is nostalgia for a primal innocence expressed in the myth of return to a natural paradise); underlines the general importance of myth in Z: 'C'est par là seulement qu'il a pu, dans son oeuvre, exprimer et surmonter ses contradictions.'

See also Bc82, 90, 348, 387.

Fécondité (1899)

Bd122   Berg, Walter Bruno, 'Der utopische Sonntag. Z: *Fécondité*', in *Der literarische Sonntag. Ein Beitrag zur Kritik der bürgerlichen Ideologie* (Studia Romanica, 25), Heidelberg: Winter, 1976, pp. 191-4.

Bd123   Field, Trevor, Refs in 'Les images de fécondité et de stérilité dans les romans patriotiques français, 1885-1914', *TLLS*, XV (1977), 143-53.

Bd124   Péguy, Charles, 'Les récentes oeuvres de Z', in *Les Cahiers de la Quinzaine*, 4e série, 5e cahier (1902), pp. 30-58; repr. in *Oeuvres en prose, 1898-1908*, Gallimard (Bibliothèque de la Pléiade), 1959, pp. 537-60.

Bd125   Steins, Martin, 'L'épisode africain de *Fécondité* et la tradition exotique', *CN*, 48 (1974), 164-81.

Bd126   ——, 'Z colonialiste', *Revue des langues vivantes*, XLI (1975), 15-30.

See also Ba29; Bb6; Bc71, 85, 144, 273, 289, 290, 312, 375.

La Fortune des Rougon (1871)

Bd127   Agulhon, M., 'Aux sources de *La Fortune des Rougon*', in Bb34, pp. 161-7.

Bd128   Chaitin, Gilbert, 'The Voices of the Dead: Love, Death and Politics in Z's *Fortune des Rougon*', *Literature and Psychology* (Fairleigh Dickinson University), XXVI (1976), 131-44, 148-58.

Bd129   Dezalay, Auguste, 'Ordre et désordre dans *Les Rougon-Mac-quart*: l'exemple de *La Fortune des Rougon*', *TLLS*, XI (1973), 71-81.
Analyses the novel's complex mixture of themes and styles (which makes it the germ of the whole cycle), the unifying role of Félicité, and the significance of its classical references, as well as its clear-cut antithetical structure.

Bd130   Gerhardi, Gerhard C., 'Z's Biological Vision of Politics: Revolutionary Figures in *La Fortune des Rougon* and *Le Ventre de Paris*', *NCFS*, II (1973-4), 164-80.
Argues that the political fervour of Sylvère and Florent springs from a kind of emotional confusion: they are so obviously suffering from sexual or nutritional deprivation that one need look no further to explain the ardour of their campaign for justice. Z's sociological explanations are by comparison weak and unconvincing. Similar patterns are discernible throughout the Rougon-Macquart cycle. Cf. Bc170, 331.

Bd131   Got, Olivier, 'L'idylle de Miette et de Silvère dans *La Fortune des Rougon*. Structure d'un mythe', *CN*, 46 (1973), 146-64.
A careful analysis of the Freudian components of the idyll.

Bd132   Grant, Elliott M., 'L'emploi de l'expédition à Rome dans *La Fortune des Rougon*', *CN*, 33 (1967), 53-6.

Bd133   Kanes, Martin, 'Z, Balzac and "La Fortune des Rogron "' [*sic*], *FS*, XVIII (1964), 203-12.
Parallels with Balzac's *Pierrette*.

Bd134   ——, '*La Fortune des Rougon* and the Thirty-third Cousin', in Bb32, pp. 36-44.
Examines the motif of enclosure and the narrator's explicit place in the narration with a view to showing that epistemological questions are basic both to *La Fortune des Rougon* and the whole Rougon-Macquart cycle; seen in terms of the philosophical position of the narrator with regard to the limits of knowledge and the possibilities of language, the *Rougon-Macquart* 'situate themselves at the leading edge of experiments in narrative devices'.

Bd135   Mitterand, Henri, 'La publication en feuilleton de *La Fortune des Rougon* (lettres inédites)', *MF*, CCCXXXVII (1959), 531-6.

Bd136   ——, 'Textes en intersection: *Le Roman expérimental* et *Les Rougon-Macquart*', in Bb95, pp. 415-28.
Argues, with particular ref. to the opening pages of *La Fortune des Rougon*,

that Z's artistic theories and novelistic practice are convergent insofar as they reflect the emergence of an ethnological type of 'realist' fiction.

Bd137   Petrey, Sandy, 'From Cyclical to Historical Discourse: The *Contes à Ninon* and *La Fortune des Rougon*', in Bb95, pp. 371-81.
Shows how minimal referential shifts effect major changes in the dramatic function of common elements.

Bd138   Raphaël, Paul, '*La Fortune des Rougon* et la réalité historique', *MF*, CLXVII (1923), 104-18.

Bd139   Ricatte, Robert, 'A propos de *La Fortune des Rougon*', *CN*, 19 (1961), 97-106; partially repr. in Ba12, pp. 135-40.
Introductory remarks on the novel's genesis, main characters, comic elements, colour symbolism, and spatial and temporal structures.

Bd140   Schor, Naomi, 'Z: From Window to Window', in Bb119, pp. 38-51; partially repr. (in French) in Ba12, pp. 106-11.
Considers the window motif as a reflection of the themes and attitudes manifested in *La Fortune des Rougon*, and suggests that the window, together with the themes of voyeurism and hereditary determinism, and Z's cyclical view of history, translate a general sense of imprisonment and individual powerlessness. Cf. Bc180, 389.

See also Bc18, 183, 332.

Germinal (1885)

Bd141   Adam, Jean-Michel, and J.-P. Goldstein, 'L'exemple du "réalisme épique": lecture d'une page de *Germinal*', in *Linguistique et discours littéraire* (Larousse universitaire, coll. L.), Larousse, 1976, pp. 168-74.

Bd142   Aubéry, Pierre, 'Quelques sources du thème de l'action directe dans *Germinal*', *S*, XIII (1959), 63-72.

Bd143   ——, 'Genèse et développement du personnage de Lantier', *FS*, XVI (1962), 142-53.

Bd144   ——, 'Faut-il récrire *Germinal*? ', *La Révolution prolétarienne*, 483 (1963), 100-4.

Bd145   ——, 'Imitations de Jésus chez Z: *Germinal*', *CN*, 53 (1979), 31-45.

Etienne Lantier seen as a Christ-figure.

Bd146   Auerbach, Erich, *Mimesis: The Representation of Reality in Western Literature*, Princeton U.P., 1953, pp. 506-15 (first pubd in German in 1946).
Describes the ways in which Z's brand of realism stands out from the aestheticism of the Goncourts, and argues (on the basis of two passages from *Germinal*) that Z contributed to the enlargement of the scope and subject-matter of the novel in that, placing emphasis on the sociological mission of the novelist, and impelled by humanitarian sympathy, he was the first French novelist to treat the working classes in their own right and on their own terms.

Bd147   Baguley, David, 'The Function of Z's Souvarine', *MLR*, LXVI (1971), 786-97.
Describes the nature and historical origins of Souvarine's nihilism, shows the narrative and allegorical relevance of his pet rabbit, Pologne, to his intellectual development (precipitating his disillusionment with his social ideals and his decision to commit himself to the inflexible assertion of his nihilism by destroying the mine and renouncing his links with humanity), and demonstrates how Etienne, by coming to accept the potentialities of life, is the antithesis of Souvarine, who may thus be seen to function primarily as 'the demonic parody of the hero of *Germinal*'.

Bd148   Bellos, David, 'From the Bowels of the Earth: An Essay on *Germinal*', *FMLS*, XV (1979), 35-45.
Argues that part of the power of *Germinal* springs from the fact that, by offering a precise and epic enactment of the fantasy of anal birth, it becomes 'an involuntary and efficient exercise in mass psychotherapy'.

Bd149   Berg, William, 'A Note on Imagery as Ideology in Z's *Germinal*', *Clio*, II (Oct. 1972), 43-5.
A footnote to Bc358: argues that the dialectical opposition between images of growth and the depiction of the miners in terms of animal images, resolved at the end of the novel by the refs to Darwin, points to a progressive and optimistic vision of the working class and of history.

Bd150   Blankenagel, John C., 'The Mob in Z's *Germinal* and in Hauptmann's *Weavers*', *PMLA*, XXXIX (1924), 705-21.
Cf. Bd198.

Bd151   Brady, Patrick, 'Structuration archétypologique de *Germinal*', *Cahiers internationaux de symbolisme*, 24-5 (1973), 87-97.
A somewhat fanciful exploration of Catherine's triple mythological function

as a sort of Persephone (fecundation), Demeter (initiation) and Ariadne (liberation).

Bd152   Chevrel, Yves, '*Germinal* et la "révolution littéraire" en Allemagne', *CN*, 50 (1976), 146-64.
On Z's influence.

Bd153   Cirillo, N.R., 'Marxism as Myth in Z's *Germinal*', *Comparative Literature Studies*, XIV (1977), 244-55.
Argues that Z's use of Marxist theory within the novel is purely literary.

Bd154   Cogny, Pierre, 'Ouverture et clôture dans *Germinal*', *CN*, 50 (1976), 67-73.

Bd155   Davoine, Jean-Pierre, 'Métaphores animales dans *Germinal*', *Etudes françaises*, IV (1968), 383-92.

Bd156   Dubois, E.T., 'Un modèle insoupçonné de Souvarine', *CN*, 40 (1970), 144-50.
The suggested model is Huysmans.

Bd157   Duchet, Claude, 'Idéologie de la mise en texte: ouverture de *Germinal*', *Dossiers pédagogiques de la R.T.S.*, II (français, 1972-3), 104-7.
Cf. Bc120, 123, 127.

Bd158   ——, 'Le trou des bouches noires. Parole, société, révolution dans *Germinal*', *Littérature*, 24 (1976), 11-39.
Sociocriticism fruitfully applied to the textual function of the spoken word in *Germinal*.

Bd159   Eoff, Sherman H., 'The Deification of Unconscious Process', in *The Modern Spanish Novel*, New York U.P., 1961, pp. 85-147 (pp. 85-109 concern Z).
Focuses on the opposition between individualism and the fusion of individual personality with mass consciousness.

Bd160   Féral, Josette, 'La sémiotique des couleurs dans *Germinal*', *CN*, 49 (1975), 136-48.

Bd161   Frandon, Ida-Marie, 'Art et pensée de Z d'après *Germinal*', *CN*, 5 (1956), 219-23.
A series of *lectures commentées*.

Bd162   Gaillard, Françoise, Refs in '*Deux heures du matin sonnèrent...*

Quelques remarques sur la temporalité dans le roman naturaliste', in Bb94, pp. 553-64.

Bd163   Geffroy, Gustave, '*Germinal*', *La Justice* (14.7.1885); repr. in *Notes d'un journaliste*, Charpentier, 1887, pp. 185-99.
A perceptive contemporary review which presents Z as a 'poète panthéiste qui sait superbement augmenter et idéaliser les choses'; complements Bc243.

Bd164   Georgin, Robert, 'Le thème du labyrinthe', in *La Structure et le style*, Lausanne: L'Age d'homme, 1975, pp. 33-9.
Remarks on the Oedipal structure of *Germinal*.

Bd165   Gerhardi, Gerhard, '*Germinal*: Mass Action and the Psychology of the Individual', *Studi di letteratura francese: 1974* (Florence: Olschki, 1975), 142-56.

Bd166   Gillet, Marcel, 'La grève d'Anzin de 1884 et *Germinal*', *CN*, 50 (1976), 59-66.

Bd167   Girard, Marcel, 'L'univers de *Germinal*', *RSH*, 69 (1953), 59-76; partially repr. in Ba12, pp. 140-52.
A seminal study which analyses *Germinal* as a unified symbolic world and illuminates brilliantly the poetic and visionary aspects of Z's talent, thus firmly establishing the legitimacy of a non-naturalistic interpretation of his novels.

Bd168   Grant, Elliott M., 'Concerning the Sources of *Germinal*', *RR*, XLIX (1958), 168-78.

Bd169   ——, 'La source historique d'une scène de *Germinal*', *RHLF*, LX (1960), 61-3.
The historical basis of the execution of Annouchka, Souvarine's wife.

Bd170   ——, 'The Newspapers of *Germinal*: Their Identity and Significance', *MLR*, LV (1960), 87-9.

Bd171   ——, 'Marriage or Murder: Z's Hesitations Concerning Cécile Grégoire', *FS*, XV (1961), 41-6.

Bd172   ——, 'Quelques précisions sur une source de *Germinal*: *La Question ouvrière au 19e siècle*, par Paul Leroy-Beaulieu', *CN*, 22 (1962), 249-54.

Bd173   ——, and Philip D. Walker, 'Concerning Color in *Germinal*', *PMLA*, LXXIX (1964), 348-54.

A dialogue provoked by Grant's reactions to Bd220; focuses on the fundamental issues of whether the poetic imagination in Z's fiction should be regarded as subordinate to the faithful imitation of reality and the extent to which interpretations of the novels should be determined by Z's stated intentions.

Bd174 ——, 'Les épreuves de *Germinal* conservées à New York', *CN*, 30 (1965), 153-7.
Comments on Bd182.

Bd175 ——, 'A Correction in the Manuscript of *Germinal*', *FR*, XXXIX (1965-6), 521-2.

Bd176 Hambly, Peter, 'La genèse de *Germinal*: les grèves et la société', *CN*, 41 (1971), 96-112.

Bd177 Hayman, David, 'The Broken Cranium — Headwounds in Z, Rilke, Céline: A Study in Contrasting Modes', *Comparative Literature Studies*, IX (1972), 207-33.
Explores the resonances and analogical value of the shattering of Chaval's skull in terms of the total context of the novel; the Rilke example is taken from *Malte Laurids*, the Céline from *Mort à crédit*; jargon tends to obscure Hayman's argument.

Bd178 Hemmings, F.W.J., 'De *Jack* à *Germinal*: le prolétaire vu par Alphonse Daudet et EZ', *CN*, 50 (1976), 107-14.
A deft analysis of parallels and differences.

Bd179 Howe, Irving, 'Z: The Genius of *Germinal*', *Encounter*, XXXIV (April 1970), 53-61; repr. as an Afterword to *Germinal*, New York: New American Library Inc., 1970, and in *The Critical Point: On Literature and Culture*, New York: Horizon Press, 1973, pp. 59-76.
A lively introduction; emphasizes that '*Germinal* releases one of the central myths of the modern era: the story of how the dumb acquire speech'.

Bd180 Joyce, Wendy, and Elizabeth Mahler Schächter, 'Giovanni Verga and EZ: A Question of Influence', *Journal of European Studies*, VII (1977), 266-77.

Bd181 Kanes, Martin, '*Germinal*: Drama and Dramatic Structure', *Modern Philology*, LXI (1963-4), 12-25.
Shows that the play *Germinal* (which was planned before the novel but written afterwards) was Z's own work and not Busnach's, and brings out,

through a careful examination of the novel's *dossier*, the ways in which the play helps to account for some of the novel's dramatic and melodramatic qualities.

Bd182   Lapp, John C., 'De nouvelles épreuves corrigées par Z: *Germinal*', *CN*, 21 (1962), 223-6.
Cf. Bd174.

Bd183   Ledig, Gerhard, 'Ein danteskes Kapitel aus Zs *Germinal*', *Deutsches Dante-Jahrbuch* (Leipzig), XXIII (1954), 87-93.

Bd184   Lejeune, Philippe, 'La Côte-Verte et le Tartaret', *Poétique*, 40 (1979), 475-86.
Close analysis of the passage on 'la Côte-Verte' and 'le Tartaret' (Part V, chapter 1) in order to bring out the ideological ambivalence of *Germinal*.

Bd185   Lindenberg, Daniel, 'Les "Mystères de Montsou", ou la critique de la raison brute', in Bb44, pp. 11-30.
An intelligent analysis of the 'non-revolutionary' assumptions implicit in Z's social vision in *Germinal*.

Bd186   Loquet, Francis, 'La documentation géographique dans *Germinal*', *RSH*, 79 (1955), 377-85.

Bd187   Malrieu, Philippe, 'Témoignage du romancier sur la psychologie ouvrière', *Journal de psychologie*, LVIII (1961), 171-91.

Bd188   Marel, Henri, 'Une source possible de *Germinal*? ', *CN*, 39 (1970), 49-60.
Suggests that Z may have drawn on a strike at Anzin in 1866 (the date of the strike in *Germinal*) as well as the strike he witnessed there in 1884.

Bd189   ——, 'A propos de *Germinal* et des *Rougon-Macquart*', *CN*, 45 (1973), 94-6.
The example of *Germinal* suggests that the links between the individual novels of the *Rougon-Macquart* series are more organic than has been imagined.

Bd190   ——, 'Etienne Lantier et les chefs syndicalistes', *CN*, 50 (1976), 26-39.
A well-researched study which shows that Z 'appréhende avec une extrême sûreté la vie d'autrui, l'atmosphère d'un univers', and that 'la documentation livresque ne fait que compléter une impression'.

Bd191   Matthews, J.H., 'The Art of Description in Z's *Germinal*', *S*, XVI

(1962), 267-74.
Shows how Z employs a descriptive technique analogous to that of the cinema in order to give physical décor and atmosphere their necessary importance while avoiding intrusion into the narrative. Cf. Bc152, 206, 344; Bd201, 326; Bf12.

Bd192   Mitterand, Henri, 'The Calvary of Catherine Maheu: The Description of a Page in *Germinal*', in Bb119, pp. 115-25.
A suggestive explication of a passage taken from Part V, chapter 2.

Bd193   ——, 'Notes sur l'idéologie du mythe dans *Germinal*', *La Pensée*, n.s., 156 (1971), 81-6; repr. in *Problèmes d'analyse textuelle*, ed. Pierre Léon et al., Montreal: Didier, 1971, pp. 83-92.
Outlines the ways in which Z naturalizes situation and action, making them mythic and eternal rather than contingent and social; the novel thus refracts late-nineteenth-century bourgeois ideology.

Bd194   ——, '*Germinal* et les idéologies', *CN*, 42 (1971), 141-52.
An amplification of the argument in Bd193.

Bd195   ——, 'Le système des personnages dans *Germinal*', in Bb19, pp. 155-66.
A strikingly successful application of structural analysis to the function of the characters within the novel's textual system.

Bd196   ——, 'Fonction narrative et fonction mimétique. Les personnages de *Germinal*', in Bb89, pp. 477-90.
Complements Bd195.

Bd197   ——, 'Poétique et idéologie: la dérivation figurale dans *Germinal*', in Grant E. Kaiser, ed., *Fiction, Form, Experience/Fiction, forme, expérience*, Montreal: Edns France-Québec, 1976, pp. 44-52.
On the fusion of the poetic resonances of the text with its ideological implications.

Bd198   Moore, Charles H., 'A Hearing on *Germinal* and *Die Weber*', *Germanic Review* (New York), XXXIII (1958), 30-40.
Cf. Bd150.

Bd199   Moreau, Pierre, 'Le *Germinal* d'Yves Guyot', *RHLF*, LIV (1954), 208-13.
Guyot's *L'Enfer social* (1882) as a 'hidden source' for *Germinal*.

Bd200   Neuschäfer, Hans-Jörg, '*Germinal*', in *Der französische Roman*.

Vom Mittelalter bis Gegenwart, II, ed. Klaus Heitmann, Düsseldorf: Bagel, 1975, pp. 9-33, 327.

Bd201   Newton, Joy, 'Z and Eisenstein', in Bb40, pp. 106-16.
Similarities between the confrontation of troops and miners in *Germinal* and the Odessa steps sequence in *Battleship Potemkin*. Cf. Bc152, 206, 344; Bd191, 326; Bf12.

Bd202   Orr, John, 'Z: *Germinal* and Tragic *Praxis*', in *Tragic Realism and Modern Society: Studies in the Sociology of the Modern Novel*, London: Macmillan, 1977, pp. 87-98.
A discussion of *Germinal* in the context of a theory of tragic realism derived from Auerbach's *Mimesis* (Bd146). The tragic realism of the novel resides in Z's recognition of the dilemma of socialist *praxis*: the working-class revolt led by Etienne is doomed to failure, but Etienne must convince the miners that their own circumstances will improve through their action, for only through this type of conviction are long-term gains for the working classes made possible. Z's portrayal of Etienne's corruption by the power of leadership and the miners' corruption by the power of violence reveal his concern with the high standards which authentic socialist values demand of the individual personality; where those values are not met, the novel expresses the tragic pity of that failure.

Bd203   Pasco, Allan H., 'Myth, Metaphor, and Meaning in *Germinal*', *FR*, XLVI (1972-3), 739-49.
Stresses the openness and ambivalence of the ending of *Germinal*. The novel suggests through its mythic structure the birth of a new man and a new race. It implies that only Etienne, or someone like him, can offer an alternative to the real menace, represented by Souvarine, of a holocaust through fire and blind destruction. The ambivalence of the book thus lies in the fact that the workers may use law, reason and justice to transform their lives, or the forces of nature will engulf all.

Bd204   Petrey, Sandy D., 'The Revolutionary Setting of Z's *Germinal*', *FR*, XLIII (1969-70), 54-63.
Demonstrates effectively how Z's fictional use of historical reality plays upon the emotions and political consciousness of his reader; the revolutionary setting of the novel thus serves him both as subject matter and as an important component of narrative technique.

Bd205   ——, 'Discours social et littérature dans *Germinal*', *Littérature*, 22 (1976), 59-74.
Penetrating structural analysis which raises some basic methodological issues concerning the political interpretation of literature and attempts to show

that Z's textual presentation of the workers in fact reveals 'une conscience révolutionnaire des rapports humains dans une société de classes'.

Bd206   Psichari, Henriette, 'L'enfant, martyr de la mine', *MF*, CCCXL (1960), 654-66.

Bd207   ——, 'La limite entre le réel et l'imaginaire dans *Germinal*', in Bb34, pp. 178-82.

Bd208   Rannaud, Gérald, 'Notes sur la structure d'un refuge: la mine dans *Germinal*', *Circé (Cahiers du Centre de recherche sur l'imaginaire)*, 3 (1972), 301-13.
On the rich mythical resonances of Le Réquillart, the abandoned mine; cf. Bc111.

Bd209   Ripoll, Roger, 'L'avenir dans *Germinal*: destruction et renaissance', *CN*, 50 (1976), 115-33.
Brings out optimistic aspects of Z's social vision.

Bd210   Rosenberg, Rachelle A., 'The Slaying of the Dragon: An Archetypal Study of Z's *Germinal*', *S*, XXVI (1972), 349-61.
Using the arguments of Neumann's *The Great Mother* and Jung's *Symbols of Transformation*, attempts to show that *Germinal* 'takes the form of sun myths in which the hero is swallowed up by night, the sea or the underworld, and in which the sun-hero emerges after having defeated the darkness'; masculine symbols of sun and light ultimately triumph over the 'Terrible Mother'.

Bd211   Roy, Claude, 'Sur *Germinal*', in *Descriptions critiques*, IV. *La Main heureuse*, Gallimard, 1958, pp. 214-24.

Bd212   Salvan, Albert J., ed., 'Un document retrouvé. "M. EZ et *Germinal*" de Henry Céard, retraduit de l'espagnol, présenté et annoté par Albert J. Salvan', *CN*, 35 (1968), 42-60.
A critical essay by Céard which first appeared in a Buenos Aires journal, *Sud-América*, in April 1885.

Bd213   Schober, Rita, 'Die Wirklichkeitssicht des *Germinal*', in *Skizzen zur Literaturtheorie*, Berlin: Deutscher Verlag der Wissenschaften, 1956, pp. 70-162.
An orthodox and rather turgid Marxist view of *Germinal* as an isolated triumph of 'realism' over Z's theories; stresses that the novel's success is inherent in its subject-matter.

Bd214   Schreiber, Till., 'Perspectivierende Elemente in Zs *Germinal*', in

Formen perspectivischer Leserführung im französischen Roman des 19. und 20. Jahrhunderts, Frankfurt am Main/Berne: Lang, 1976, pp. 102-11.

Bd215   Ternois, René, Review of Bb47, *CN*, 23 (1963), 316-19.

Bd216   Tersen, Emile, 'Sources et sens de *Germinal*', *La Pensée*, n.s., 95 (1961), 74-89.

Bd217   Topazio, Virgil W., 'A Study of Motion in *Germinal*', *Kentucky Foreign Language Quarterly*, XIII, Supplement (1967), 60-70.
Z's use of motion both heightens the novel's dramatic effects and reinforces the author's socialistic ideas.

Bd218   Troy, William, 'The Symbolism of Z', *Partisan Review*, IV (1937), 64-6.
On the mythic dimension of *Germinal*.

Bd219   Vissière, Jean-Louis, 'Politique et prophétie dans *Germinal*', *CN*, 20 (1962), 166-7.
Germinal illustrates the powerfully synthetic nature of Z's imagination by blending a myth of decadence with Marxist and Darwinian elements.

Bd220   Walker, Philip D., 'Z's Use of Color Imagery in *Germinal*', *PMLA*, LXXVII (1962), 442-9.
A careful analysis of Z's symbolic treatment of colour; cf. Bd173.

Bd221   ——, 'Z's Art of Characterization in *Germinal*: A Note for Further Research', *L'Esprit créateur*, IV (Summer 1964), 60-7.
Penetrating observations on Z's techniques of presenting character; his characters are to be appreciated in terms of their effectiveness as symbols rather than as lifelike representations.

Bd222   ——, 'The *Ebauche* of *Germinal*', *PMLA*, LXXX (1965), 571-83.
A meticulous analysis of the *Ebauche*, describing the various stages it represents in the planning of the novel, its general role in the novel's elaboration ('a methodical translation of a general social scientific thesis into dramatic terms'), the different kinds of mental activity involved (scientific, poetic, etc.), and how little it reveals of Z's creative genius.

Bd223   ——, 'Remarques sur l'image du serpent dans *Germinal*', *CN*, 31 (1966), 83-5.
Although not one of the central metaphors of *Germinal*, the recurring image of a snake clearly illustrates an important aspect of Z's poetic imagination: the transformation of realistic material into poetic vision without the

laws of naturalistic *vraisemblance* being violated.

Bd224 ——, '*Germinal* et la pensée religieuse de Z', *CN*, 50 (1976), 134-45.
Highlights the religious resonances of Z's world-view in *Germinal*; cf. Bd46.

Bd225 Woollen, Geoff, '*Germinal*: une vie d'insecte', *CN*, 50 (1976), 97-106.
A lucid examination of the social connotations of the insect motif.

Bd226 Zimmerman, Melvin, 'L'homme et la nature dans *Germinal*', *CN*, 44 (1972), 212-18.

See also Bb1, 26, 37, 41, 43, 44, 45, 47, 69, 71, 83, 92, 106, 112, 113, 117, 120; Bc125, 169, 170, 198, 243, 268, 295, 309, 358, 379, 387, 408, 411, 413; Bd20, 40, 62, 117; Be35; Bf60.

La Joie de vivre (1884)

Bd227 Alcorn, Clayton, Jr, 'Z's Forgotten Spokesman: Véronique in *La Joie de vivre*', *FR*, XLIX (1975-6), 76-80.
An investigation of the role of Véronique, the servant, undermines recent assumptions that *La Joie de vivre*, true to its title, reveals a basically optimistic outlook.

Bd228 Baguley, David, 'De la mer ténébreuse à l'eau maternelle: le décor symbolique de *La Joie de vivre*', *TLLS*, XII (1974), 79-91.
A Bachelardian analysis of the 'symbole primordial' of the sea as the expression of the basic psychological and metaphysical themes of *La Joie de vivre*; concludes that 'Z a placé son roman au coeur de l'ambivalence fondamentale qui s'attache au symbole de la mer' (death, destruction, despair/life, hope, renewal).

Bd229 Borie, Jean, 'La Joie de vivre' and 'Conclusion: Le Tyran timide', in *Le Tyran timide. Le Naturalisme de la femme au XIXe siècle*, Klincksieck, 1973, pp. 53-156, 157-60.
A detailed analysis of *La Joie de vivre* forms the basis of a sophisticated and far-reaching study of the contradictions in the treatment of women in the works of some apparently feminist nineteenth-century writers; brings out Lazare's ambiguously despotic attitude towards the maternal figures in the novel.

Bd230 Girard, Marcel, 'EZ ou la joie de vivre', *Aesculape*, n.s., XXXIII

(1952), 198-203.
Neurotic aspects of Z's personality as reflected in Lazare Chanteau ('l'incarnation de tout ce qu'il eut à vaincre en lui-même').

Bd231   Hemmings, F.W.J., 'The Genesis of Z's *Joie de vivre*', *FS*, VI (1952), 114-25.

Bd232   Kuhn, Reinhard, 'Lazare (1884)', in *The Demon of Noontide: Ennui in Western Literature*, Princeton U.P., 1976, pp. 269-76.

Bd233   Niess, Robert J., 'Autobiographical Elements in Z's *La Joie de vivre*', *PMLA*, LVI (1941), 1133-49.

Bd234   ———, 'Z's *La Joie de vivre* and *La Mort d'Olivier Bécaille*', *MLN*, LVII (1942), 205-7.
Z's neurotic fear of death reflected in these two works.

Bd235   ———, 'Z's *La Joie de vivre* and the Opera *Lazare*', *RR*, XXXIV (1943), 223-7.

Bd236   ———, 'Z's Final Revisions of *La Joie de vivre*', *MLN*, LVIII (1943), 537-9.

Bd237   Paisse, Jean-Marie, 'L'éducation sexuelle de Pauline Quenu dans *La Joie de vivre*', *CN*, 41 (1971), 35-41.
The healthy self-education in sexual matters of Pauline Quenu is contrasted with the disastrously artificial education and harmful romantic reading of Marie Pichon in *Pot-Bouille*.

Bd238   Ternois, René, 'Les sources italiennes de *la Joie de vivre*', *CN*, 33 (1967), 27-38.

See also Bb39; Bc357, 384; Bd112.

Lourdes (1894)

Bd239   Barrès, Maurice, 'L'enseignement de *Lourdes*', *Le Figaro* (15.9.189

Bd240   Bloy, Léon, 'Le crétin des Pyrénées', *MF*, XII (Sept. 1894), 1-12; repr. in *Je m'accuse... Vignettes et culs-de-lampe de Léon Bloy*, La Maison d'art, 1900, pp. 13-41.
Violently hostile and very verbose.

Bd241   Cogny, Pierre, 'Z et Huysmans pèlerins à Lourdes', *Le Lingue*

Straniere, VII (Nov.-Dec. 1958), 18-23.
Describes the contrasting reactions of Z and Huysmans to the 'phenomenon' of Lourdes.

Bd242 Fraser, Elizabeth M., *Le Renouveau religieux d'après le roman français de 1886 à 1914*, Les Belles Lettres, 1934, pp. 180-2.

Bd243 McCrossen, Vincent A., 'Z, Werfel and the Song of Bernadette', *Renascence* (Milwaukee), XIV (1961), 34-40.
A Catholic critique.

See also Bb109; Bc144, 218, 240, 268, 289, 290, 375, 401; Bf75.

Madeleine Férat (1868)

Bd244 Bertrand-Jennings, Chantal, '*Madeleine Férat* ou les lieux ennemis', in Bb95, pp. 407-14.
Focuses on topographical constriction.

Bd245 Lapp, John C., 'Z et *la Tentation de Saint Antoine*', *RSH*, 92 (1958), 513-18; partially repr. in Bb65.
On Z's use of 'Temptation' scenes in *Madeleine Férat* and *Nana* to convey the theme of the Fatal Woman as an unconscious instrument of fate, and the possible influence of a painting of the Temptation of Saint Anthony by Cézanne.

Bd246 Walter, Rodolphe, 'Pyrame et Thisbe à l'Hôtel du Grand Cerf', *Les Nouvelles de l'Estampe*, 9 (1963), 238-41.
Echoes of the Pyramus and Thisbe myth in *Madeleine Férat*.

See also Bb65; Bc183, 232; Bd65.

Les Mystères de Marseille (1867)

Bd247 Busquet, Raoul, 'Les sources des *Mystères de Marseille*', *Provence historique*, III, 13 (July-Sept. 1953), 217-24.

Bd248 Guedj, Aimé, '*Les Mystères de Marseille* ou l'acte de naissance du naturalisme de Z', *CN*, 35 (1968), 1-19.
Intelligent analysis of the ways in which *Les Mystères de Marseille*, although artistically mediocre, provides insights into some basic features of the ideology, creative methods and poetic vision of Z's mature work.

Bd249   Ripoll, Roger, 'La publication en feuilleton des *Mystères de Mar-seille*', *CN*, 37 (1969), 20-8.

See also Bb65; Be26.

Nana (1880)

Bd250   Auriant, L., 'Les dessous de *Nana* (documents inédits)', *L'Esprit français*, VI, 72-3 (1932), 147-51, 247-51.

Bd251   ——, 'Quelques sources ignorées de *Nana*', *MF*, CCLII (1934), 180-8.

Bd252   ——, 'Les sources de *Nana*', *MF*, CCLIII (1934), 444-6.

Bd253   ——, 'Une autre source ignorée de *Nana*', *MF*, CCLIV (1934), 223-4.

Bd254   ——, '*Venise sauvée* ou les débiteurs découverts', *MF*, CCLVIII (1935), 297-308.
The scene in which Muffat is forced to imitate various animals is derived from Otway's Jacobean melodrama *Venice Preserv'd*.

Bd255   ——, 'Balzac et Z', *La France active*, 159 (1937), 100-8.
Mainly concerned with a comparison between Nana and Balzac's Mme Marneffe (*La Cousine Bette*).

Bd256   Barthes, Roland, 'La mangeuse d'hommes', *Guilde du livre. Bulletin mensuel* (Lausanne), XX (1955), 226-8.
Defines the senses in which *Nana* is an 'epic' novel, and concludes that: 'Loin de nous endormir en nous décrivant comme tant de romanciers une sorte d'épisode à peine historicisé de la Femme éternelle, éternellement mangeuse d'hommes, Z pose devant nous ce fait prétendu universel dans sa particularité historique. Et nous cessons de soupirer pour commencer à juger. Nous comprenons mieux alors la fin de cet art épique: en ramenant l'humain dans l'Histoire, l'artiste nous invite à en prendre une conscience active.'

Bd257   Braun, Sidney D., 'Z's Esthetic Approach and the Courtesan', *MLN*, LXII (1947), 449-56.
Z's approach to *la fille* is not sensation-seeking but moralistic.

Bd258   Buvik, Per, 'Nana et les hommes', *CN*, 49 (1975), 105-24.
A study of Oedipal patterns; focuses on Muffat and Georges Hugon.

Bd259   Clark, Roger J.B., '*Nana* ou l'envers du rideau', *CN*, 45 (1973), 50-64.
Nana seen as a kind of 'reprise métaphorique' of the themes of Z's drama criticism in the years immediately preceding the novel's composition.

Bd260   Conroy, Peter V., Jr, 'The Metaphorical Web in Z's *Nana*', *University of Toronto Quarterly*, XLVII (1978), 239-58.
A thorough rehearsal of the familiar view that Nana is elevated to a mythic dimension.

Bd261   Delas, Daniel, 'Etude de vocabulaire. Les unités de compte dans *Nana*', *CN*, 35 (1968), 34-41.

Bd262   Descotes, Maurice, 'Les comédiens dans les *Rougon-Macquart*', *Revue d'histoire du théâtre*, X (1958), 128-37.

Bd263   Dufay, Pierre, '*Nana* et Blanche d'Antigny', *Intermédiaire des chercheurs et des curieux*, XCVI (1933), 502-4.

Bd264   Duncan, Phillip A., 'Genesis of the Longchamp Scene in Z's *Nana*', *MLN*, LXXV (1960), 684-9.

Bd265   Jaeggy, Elena, 'Vers une lecture mythologique du roman (1)', *Rencontres artistiques et littéraires*, 5 (June 1972), 23-8.
An analysis of the mythical connotations of *Nana* which uses the methodology developed by Gilbert Durand in *Les Structures anthropologiques de l'imaginaire*; cf. Bd78.

Bd266   James, Henry, '*Nana*', *The Parisian* (26.2.1880); repr. in *The House of Fiction*, ed. Leon Edel, London: Hart-Davis, 1957, pp. 274-80, and in George J. Becker, ed., *Documents of Modern Literary Realism*, Princeton U.P., 1963, pp. 236-43.
Denounces Z for 'the singular foulness of his imagination', his tastelessness, and his lack of both humour and psychological penetration.

Bd267   Jennings, Chantal, 'Les trois visages de *Nana*', in Bb40, pp. 117-28.
A good account of Nana's multiple role as prostitute, allegorical figure and instrument of social vengeance. Cf. Bb12; Bd269.

Bd268   ——, 'La symbolique de l'espace dans *Nana*', *MLN*, LXXXVIII (1973), 764-74.
Good analysis of the ways in which the spatial structures of *Nana* reflect the basic theme of the corruption of high society by the *demi-monde*.

Bd269   ——, 'Lecture idéologique de *Nana*', *Mosaic*, X (Summer 1977),

47-54.
Nana seen again as allegorical symbol of destructive sexuality, social corruption and proletarian/feminist revolt. Cf. Bb12; Bd267.

Bd270   Lapp, John C., 'The Jealous Window-Watcher in Z and Proust', *FS*, XXIX (1975), 166-76.
Adds little to Bc231.

Bd271   Leonard, Frances McNeely, '*Nana*: Symbol and Action', *Modern Fiction Studies*, IX (1963), 149-58.
Good analysis of the ways in which the novel's controlling form and thematic coherence are provided by the symbol of the theatre and the motif of play-acting.

Bd272   Matthews, J.H., 'Une source possible de *Nana*? *Le Ménage parisien*, de Restif de la Bretonne', *CN*, 12 (1959), 504-6.

Bd273   Noaro, Jean, '*Nana*', in Bb33, pp. 111-17.

Bd274   Pagès, Alain, 'Rouge, jaune, vert, bleu. Etude du système des couleurs dans *Nana*', *CN*, 49 (1975), 125-35.

Bd275   Ternois, René, 'En marge de *Nana*', *CN*, 21 (1962), 218-22.
Some comments suggested by Henri Mitterand's notes in the Pléiade edition of *Les Rougon-Macquart*, vol. II.

Bd276   Vauzat, Guy, 'Nana et Blanche d'Antigny', *La Grand Revue*, CXL (1933), 443-56.

See also Bb5, 26, 56, 63, 65; Bc9, 90, 232, 258, 316, 357, 379; Bd34, 245; Be21.

L'Oeuvre (1886)

Bd277   Audiat, Pierre, *La Biographie de l'oeuvre littéraire. Esquisse d'une méthode critique*, Champion, 1924, pp. 178-87.
On the genesis of *L'Oeuvre*.

Bd278   Brady, Patrick, 'Symbolic Structures of Mediation and Conflict in Z's Fiction: From *Une Farce* to *Madame Sourdis* to *L'Oeuvre*', *Sub-Stance* (Madison, Wisconsin), 2 (Winter 1971-2), 85-92.

Bd279   ——, 'Pour une nouvelle orientation en sémiotique: à propos de *L'Oeuvre* d'EZ', *Rice University Studies*, LXIII (1977), 43-84.

A stimulating essay which attempts to integrate structuralist and traditionalist criticism.

Bd280 Brunius, Teddy, 'Novels in Action', in *Mutual Aid in the Arts from the Second Empire to Fin de Siècle*, Uppsala: Almqvist & Wicksell, 1972, pp. 111-53 (pp. 135-48 concern Z).
Discusses *L'Oeuvre* as a defence of Naturalism and an attack on the new spiritualism, pessimism, decadence and aestheticism of the mid-eighties.

Bd281 Carol-Bérard, 'L'Intelligence musicale de Z', *La Revue mondiale*, CLV (1923), 187-92.
The character of Gagnière reveals Z's understanding of and enthusiasm for music.

Bd282 Garland, D., 'Réminiscences de *L'Education sentimentale* dans *l'Oeuvre* d'EZ', *Les Amis de Flaubert*, 41 (1972), 35-40.

Bd283 Laubriet, Pierre, 'Z et *l'Oeuvre*', in *Un Catéchisme esthétique: 'Le chef-d'oeuvre inconnu' de Balzac*, Didier, 1961, pp. 129-50.

Bd284 Niess, Robert J., 'Z's *L'Oeuvre* and the *Reconquista* of Gamboa', *PMLA*, LXI (1946), 577-83.
Z's probable influence on the leading exponent of literary naturalism in Mexico.

Bd285 ——, 'Another View of Z's *L'Oeuvre*', *RR*, XXXIX (1948), 282-300.
A detailed discussion of the relationship between *L'Oeuvre* and Balzac's *Le Chef d'oeuvre inconnu*.

Bd286 ——, 'Henry James and Z: A Parallel', *RLC*, XXX (1956), 93-8.
The Madonna of the Future as a partial source for *L'Oeuvre*; partially repr. in Bb85.

Bd287 ——, 'Antithesis and *Reprise* in Z's *L'Oeuvre*', *L'Esprit créateur*, IV (Summer 1964), 68-75.

Bd288 ——, 'George Moore and EZ Again', *S*, XX (1966).
The scene in which Christine poses in the nude for Claude was possibly imitated from *A Modern Lover*.

Bd289 Olrik, Hilde, 'Oeil lésé, corps morcelé. Réflexions à propos de *l'Oeuvre* d'EZ', *Revue romane*, XI (1976), 334-57.
An analysis of the motifs that define the unconscious structuration of the text.

Bd290   Pasco, Allan H., 'The Failure of *L'Oeuvre*', in Bb32, pp. 45-55.
Argues that the *thèse* overpowers the *roman*'.

Bd291   Pritchett, V.S., *Books in General*, London: Chatto & Windus,
1953, pp. 110-16.

Bd292   Schober, Rita, 'Z, sein Roman *Das Werk* und der französische
Impressionismus', in *Von der wirklichen Welt in der Dichtung.
Aufsätze zur Theorie und Praxis des Realismus in der französ-
ischen Literatur*, Berlin/Weimar: Aufbau, 1970, pp. 214-47.

Bd293   Steinmetz, Jean-Luc, 'L'Oeuvre', in Bb84, pp. 415-31.
A psychocritical reading.

Bd294   Ternois, René, 'La naissance de *l'Oeuvre*', *CN*, 17 (1961), 1-9.
On Z's sources and preparatory notes.

Bd295   Zamparelli, Thomas, 'Z and the Quest for the Absolute in Art',
in Bb119, pp. 143-58.
Argues that the novel centres on the theme of authenticity in art and describes the moral and psychological make-up of the true artist: authentic
artists (Claude, Sandoz) are characterized by an obsessive attitude towards
their craft, a desire for comprehensive vision, dangerously demiurgic aspirations, a passion for the poetry of modern life, and a unanimistic world-view;
stresses that the originality of *L'Oeuvre* lies in its portrayal of the agonies
of artistic creation.

See also Bb14, 26, 63, 79, 85; Bc250, 274, 285, 300, 327, 328,
329, 384, 395, 396, 397, 398; Bf13, 14, 16, 17, 20, 23, 26, 33,
37, 38, 49, 62, 63, 84.

Une Page d'amour (1878)

Bd296   Nelson, Brian, 'Z and the Ambiguities of Passion: *Une Page
d'amour*', *Essays in French Literature*, 10 (1973), 1-22.
A structural analysis which attempts to show that as a study in sexual
psychology the novel is significant for its totally equivocal stance towards
both libidinal sexuality and bourgeois marriage.

See also Bb63; Bc9, 357.

Paris (1898)

Bd297   Blum, Léon, 'EZ: *Paris*', *La Revue blanche*, XV (1898), 551-4.
'...Il y a bien de l'illusion et une sorte de fétichisme à attendre docilement de la science le renouvellement de la Société'.

Bd298   Boudry, Robert, '*Paris*, par M. EZ', in Bb33, pp. 90-5.

Bd299   Brunetière, Ferdinand, 'Revue littéraire. Le *Paris* de M. EZ', *RDM*, CXLVI (1898), 922-34.

Bd300   Cassaing, Jean-Claude, 'Z et le drapeau noir (Du cabaret de *l'Assommoir* à l'affaire Dreyfus)', *Travaux et mémoires. Littérature française, littérature comparée (Publications de l'U.E.R. [Unité d'enseignement et de recherche] des lettres et sciences humaines de Limoges)*, 1 (May 1973), 69-103.
On Z's treatment of anarchist ideology in *Paris*.

Bd301   Faguet, Emile, 'EZ: *Paris*', in *Propos littéraires*, Société française d'imprimerie et de librairie, 1902, pp. 257-66.

Bd302   Jaurès, Jean, 'Tribune libre. Science et socialisme', *La Lanterne* (20.3.1898).
A critique of Z's confidence in science; science without militant socialist action will never create a better society.

Bd303   Niess, Robert J., 'Z's *Paris* and the Novels of the *Rougon-Macquart* Series', *NCFS*, IV (1975-6), 89-104.
A thorough account of elements borrowed or imitated from earlier novels.

Bd304   Theis, Raimund, 'Paris-Rom bei Z', in *Zur Sprache der 'Cité' in der Dichtung. Untersuchungen zum Roman und zum Prosagedicht. Realismusstudien*, I. *Teil (Analectica Romanica*, Heft 33), Frankfurt am Main: Klostermann, 1972, pp. 74-93.

See also Bb38, 63, 79, 109; Bc137, 144, 166, 218, 240, 272, 289, 290, 375, 401.

Pot-Bouille (1882)

Bb305   Brunetière, Ferdinand, 'A propos de *Pot-Bouille*', *RDM* (15.5.1882), 454-65; repr. in Bc56, pp. 347-68.

Z's most representative bourgeois critic attacks Z for producing a mere caricature of the bourgeoisie.

Bd306   Grant, Elliott M., 'The Political Scene in Z's *Pot-Bouille*', *FS*, VIII (1954), 342-7.

Bd307   Hamon, Philippe, 'Le personnage de l'abbé Mauduit dans *Pot-Bouille*: sources et thèmes', *CN*, 44 (1972), 201-11.

Bd308   Nelson, Brian, 'Black Comedy: Notes on Z's *Pot-Bouille*', *Romance Notes*, XVII (Winter 1976), 156-61.
Argues that it is satiric fantasy and the dramatic mode which define the structure and tone of *Pot-Bouille*.

Bd309   ——, 'Z and the Bourgeoisie: A Reading of *Pot-Bouille*', *NFS*, XVII (May 1978), 58-70.
A study of the social vision that emerges from Z's satire on bourgeois sexuality.

Bd310   Ten Brink, Jan, *'Pot-Bouille'*, in *Nieuwe Romans*, Haarlem: Tjeenk Willink, 1883, pp. 83-112.
Cf. Bb108; Bd52.

See also Bb63; Bc9, 377; Bd237; Be32.

Le Rêve (1888)

Bd311   Grant, Elliott M., 'The Bishop's Role in Z's *Le Rêve*', *RR*, LIII (1962), 105-11.

Bd312   Matthews, J.H., 'Z's *Le Rêve* as an Experimental Novel', *MLR*, LII (1957), 187-94.
Le Rêve was not a concession to public opinion after the 'obscenities' of *La Terre* but a transference of the experimental method to another level of society.

Bd313   Skwarczynska, Stefania, 'Un cas particulier d'orchestration générique de l'oeuvre littéraire', in *To Honor Roman Jakobson. Essays on the Occasion of his Seventieth Birthday*, III, The Hague: Mouton, 1967, pp. 1832-56.
Le Rêve considered in conjunction with Robbe-Grillet's *La Jalousie*.

See also Bc90, 110; Bf75.

Rome (1896)

Bd314   Arrighi, Paul, 'Z à Rome (1894)', *RLC*, VIII (1928), 488-99.

Bd315   Faguet, Emile, 'EZ: *Rome*', in *Propos littéraires*, Société française d'imprimerie et de librairie, 1902, pp. 237-55.

Bd316   Menichelli, Gian Carlo, 'Una fonte poco nota del romanzo *Rome*
di EZ', in *Studi sulla letteratura dell'ottocento in onore di Pietro
Paolo Trompeo*, Naples: Edizioni Scientifiche Italiane, 1959, pp.
390-401.

Bd317   Sperco, Willy, 'EZ à Rome', in Bb90, pp. 50-4.

Bd318   Ternois, René, 'La genèse du premier chapitre de *Rome*', in *Mélanges de linguistique et de littérature romanes offerts à Mario
Roques*, III, Didier, 1952, pp. 265-73.

Bd319   Trompeo, Pietro Paolo, 'La Rome de Z', in Bb90, pp. 42-9.

Bd320   Villefosse, Louis de, '*Rome*', in Bb33, pp. 74-85.

See also Bb109; Bc106, 144, 218, 240, 289, 290, 375, 401; Bd304.

Son Excellence Eugène Rougon (1876)

Bd321   Bergeron, Régis, 'Pour faire lire *Son Excellence Eugène Rougon*,
le livre le moins lu d'EZ', in Bb33, pp. 99-107.

Bd322   Grant, Elliott M., 'Studies on Z's *Son Excellence Eugène Rougon*',
RR, XLIV (1953), 24-39.
On Z's sources for the attempted assassination of Louis-Napoleon (Chapter
VIII) and the legislative debate described in the final chapter.

See also Bb49, 63; Bc129, 232; Bd70.

La Terre (1887)

Alas, Leopoldo: see Bd327.

Bd323   Brachet, Pierre, 'Z et Hauptmann. *Rose Bernd* et *la Terre*', *CN*,
49 (1975), 149-67.

Bd324   Brunetière, Ferdinand, 'La banqueroute du naturalisme', *RDM*, LXXXIII (1887), 213-24; repr. in Bc56 (1892 edn), pp. 345-68.

Bd325   Cesbron, Georges, '*La Terre* de Z: capitalisme ou socialisme? ', *Les Humanités* (Classes de lettres, Sections modernes), XIV (June 1971), 18-23.

An analysis of the ways in which 'la situation dramatique' and 'la mise en disposition des personnages' reflect a dialectical and genetic structure which dramatizes the ideological confrontation of capitalism and socialism.

Bd326   Clamens, Pierre A., 'Style descriptif chez Loti et chez Z – Perspective statique et perspective cinétique', *MLN*, LXXIV (1959), 521-30.

Cf. Bc152, 206; Bd191, 201; Bf12.

Bd327   Clarín (Leopoldo Alas), 'Z. *La Terre*', in *Ensayos y revistas, 1888-1892*, Madrid: Manuel Fernández y Lasanta, 1892, pp. 31-55.

An admiring review.

Bd328   Donnard, Jean-Hervé, '*Les Paysans* et *la Terre*', *L'Année balzacienne 1975*, Garnier, 1975, 125-42.

Bd329   Duncan, Phillip A., 'Z's "An Election at Villebranche" ', *S*, XV (1961), 286-96.

Gives the text (in English translation) of an article Z wrote for *Vestnik Evropy*, in which he denounces the pressures brought to bear on rural electors; the issue is reflected in *La Terre*.

Bd330   France, Anatole, '*La Terre*', *Le Temps* (28.8.1887); repr. in *La Vie littéraire*, première série, Calmann Lévy, 1889, pp. 225-38.

A celebrated attack: 'En écrivant *la Terre*, [Z] a donné les Georgiques de la crapule.'

Bd331   Gruau, Georges, 'A propos de *La Terre* de Z', *MF*, CCLXXI (1936), 640-8.

Shows from documentary sources that even the most horrific scenes in the novel are based on actual occurrence.

Bd332   Harvey, Lawrence E., 'The Cycle Myth in *La Terre* of Z', *Philological Quarterly*, XXXVIII (1959), 89-95.

A perceptive analysis of the theme of circular movement in *La Terre*, which suggests that Z's use of the myth of eternal return had a more profound influence on the structure of the novel than Robert implies in Bb99, pp.385-8.

Bd333 Legouis, Emile, '*La Terre* de Z et le *Roi Lear*', *RLC*, XXVII (1953), 417-27.
The text of a lecture originally given in 1889.

Bd334 Marcilhacy, Christiane, 'EZ "historien" des paysans beaucerons', *Annales*, XII (1957), 573-86.
Extensively illustrates the authenticity of Z's depiction of the 1850 peasantry.

Bd335 Olorenshaw, Robert, 'Lisibilité, structures globales et méta-discours critique dans *La Terre*', *CN*, 53 (1979), 46-52.

Bd336 Pageard, Robert, '*La Terre* vue par la presse d'Eure-et-Loir lors de sa publication (1887-1888)', *CN*, 40 (1970), 177-85.

Bd337 Sutton, Geneviève, 'Au pays de *La Terre*', *FR*, XLI (1967-8), 232-42.
On Z's visits to models for the setting of his novel.

Bd338 Vernois, Paul, *Le Roman rustique de George Sand à Ramuz: ses tendances et son évolution (1860-1925)*, Nizet, 1962, pp. 130-43.

Bd339 Zakarian, Richard H., 'Z's *La Terre*', *The Explicator*, XXXVI (Winter 1978), 11-13.
Analyses Part IV, chapter 4, of *La Terre* in order to illustrate Z's use of ribald humour to delineate the moral and religious hypocrisy of both peasantry and bourgeoisie.

See also Bb43, 67, 99, 114; Bc309, 379, 413; Bd353.

Thérèse Raquin (1867)

Bd340 Atkins, Stuart, 'A possible Dickens Influence in Z', *MLQ*, VIII (1947), 302-8.
Possible reflections of the paralyzed Mrs Clennam (*Little Dorrit*) in Madame Raquin.

Bd341 Claverie, Michel, '*Thérèse Raquin*, ou les Atrides dans la boutique du Pont-Neuf', *CN*, 36 (1968), 138-47.

Bd342 Dugan, R., 'La psychologie criminelle dans *Thérèse Raquin* et *La Bête humaine* d'EZ', *TLLS*, XVII (1979), 131-7.

Bd343 Ferragus [Louis Ulbach], 'La littérature putride', *Le Figaro* (23.1.1868).
A violently hostile review which charged Z with gross immorality.

Bd344 Furst, Lilian R., 'Z's *Thérèse Raquin*: A Re-Evaluation', *Mosaic*, V (Spring 1972), 189-202.
A lucid demonstration that *Thérèse Raquin* is by no means the straight-forward prototype of Naturalism that it is generally assumed to be: in both presentation and content, the novel often departs radically from the doctrinal Naturalism outlined in Z's preface to the second edn (1868).

Bd345 ——, 'A Question of Choice in the Naturalistic Novel: Z's *Thérèse Raquin* and Dreiser's *An American Tragedy*', in Wolodymyr T. Zyla and Wendell M. Aycock, eds, *Proceedings of the Comparative Literature Symposium*, V: *Modern American Fiction. Insights and Foreign Lights*, Lubbock: Texas Tech. Univ., 1972, pp. 39-53.
Shows that the main characters, although obviously moulded by temperament and environment, are capable of exercising a conscious choice at key moments of the narrative; fortunately, the vast discrepancies in Naturalist theory and practice work to the advantage of the latter.

Bd346 Guiches, Gustave, 'Le Manifeste des Cinq', in *Au Banquet de la vie*, Spes, 1925, pp. 216-36.

Bd347 Jennings, Chantal, '*Thérèse Raquin*, ou le péché originel', *Littérature*, 23 (1976), 94-101.
A penetrating study of Z's development of the theme of sexual guilt.

Bd348 Kanes, Martin, 'Autour de *Thérèse Raquin*: un dialogue entre Z et Sainte-Beuve', *CN*, 31 (1966), 23-31.
An exchange of letters (1868-9) between Sainte-Beuve and Z, centring on the former's criticisms of Z's psychological depiction of his protagonists.

Bd349 Mandin, Louis, 'Les origines de *Thérèse Raquin*', *MF*, CCXCVII (1940), 282-98.

Bd350 Mitterand, Henri, 'Corrélations lexicales et organisation du récit: le vocabulaire du visage dans *Thérèse Raquin*', in *La Nouvelle Critique*, numéro spécial: *Linguistique et littérature* (Colloque de Cluny, April 1968), 1968, pp. 21-8.
An exercise in semiological analysis which demonstrates that such an approach to Z may yield fruitful results.

Bd351 Niess, Robert J., 'Hawthorne and Z — an Influence? ', *RLC*, XXVII (1953), 446-52

Ulbach, Louis: see Bd343.

Bd352   Walter, Rodolphe, 'Z à Bennecourt en 1867. Quelques aperçus nouveaux sur *Thérèse Raquin*', *CN*, 30 (1965), 119-31.
The possible influence of the region of Bennecourt.

Bd353   ——, 'Z à Bennecourt en 1867. *Thérèse Raquin* vingt ans avant *La Terre*', *CN*, 33 (1967), 12-26.

See also Bb65; Bc9, 183; Be21, 25.

Travail (1901)

Bd354   Chevrel, Yves, 'Questions de méthodes et d'idéologies chez Verne et Z: *Les Cinq cents millions de la Bégum* et *Travail*', in *Jules Verne 2. L'Ecriture vernienne*. Textes réunis par François Raymond, *Revue des lettres modernes*, Minard, 1978, pp. 69-96.

Bd355   Desroche, Henri, 'De Charles Fourier à EZ. Aspects de l'humanisme phalanstérien', *Communauté*, VIII (Oct.-Nov. 1953), 15-20.

Bd356   ——, 'De Charles Fourier à EZ. Aspects de l'utopisme phalanstérien', *Communauté*, VIII (Dec. 1953), 23-31.

Bd357   ——, 'De Charles Fourier à EZ ou l'utopie ré-écrite', in *La Société festive. Du fouriérisme écrit aux fouriérismes pratiqués*, Seuil, 1975, pp. 321-46.

Bd358   Greaves, A.A., 'EZ and the Danger of Optimism', *Pacific Coast Philology* (Northridge, California), IV (April 1969), 37-40.
Argues that Z's views of a new society are an interesting throwback to the eighteenth century, because they rely on the same view of man. Moreover, Z's liberty, like the liberty envisaged by eighteenth-century thinkers, becomes a most repressive egalitarianism if there is any suspicion that man's desires may conflict with the wishes of the state; and, like eighteenth-century thinkers, Z contented himself with repeating that man was fundamentally good and altruistic, without seeking to justify his statements.

Bd359   Jaurès, Jean, 'Conférence sur *Travail* d'EZ', *Revue socialiste*, XXXII (1901), 641-53; repr. as *Le Travail*, Bibliothèque ouvrière socialiste, 1901.
Reproaches Z with minimizing the role of the workers in the creation of a socialist society.

Bd360   ——, '*Travail*', *La Petite République* (23.4.1901 and 25.4.1901).

Repeats the views expressed in Bb359.

Bd361 Mitterand, Henri, 'L'évangile social de *Travail*: un anti-*Germinal*', *Mosaic*, V (Spring 1972), 179-87; repr. in *Roman et société*, Armand Colin, 1973, pp. 74-83.
The content and structure of *Germinal* (1885) and *Travail* (1901) reflect contrasting solutions to class warfare: confrontation and cooperation. While *Germinal* is based on dramatic tensions and oppositions, *Travail* is informed by a sense of natural, linear progression; similarly, the rejection of the idea of violent change is matched by the replacement of proletarian strikers by bourgeois reformers.

Bd362 Naumont, Josiane, 'Enquête sur une visite de Z à Unieux pour la préparation de *Travail*', *CN*, 48 (1974), 182-204.

See also Ba29; Bb22; Bc71, 85, 137, 144, 273, 289, 290, 312, 375, 411.

Le Ventre de Paris (1873)

Bd363 Baguley, David, 'Le supplice de Florent: à propos du *Ventre de Paris*', in Bb34, pp. 91-6.
An analysis of Florent's inability to resist engulfment by matter.

Bd364 Engler, Winfried, 'Idyllen bei Z und Vailland', *Zeitschrift für französische Sprache und Literatur* (Wiesbaden), LXXII (1962), 147-54.
A comparison with *La Loi*.

Bd365 Matthews, J.H., 'L'impressionnisme chez Z: *Le Ventre de Paris*', *Le Français moderne*, XXIX (1961), 199-205.
A useful examination of Z's descriptive impressionism; cf. Bc173, 269, 296, 297, 298.

Bd366 Petrey, Sandy, 'Historical Reference and Stylistic Opacity in *Le Ventre de Paris*', *Kentucky Romance Quarterly* (Lexington), XXIV (1977), 325-40.
Penetrating analysis of the ways in which historical information and stylistic patterns constantly interact with and reinforce one another.

See also Bd26, 63, 79; Bc82, 379, 408; Bd130; Be32.

Vérité (1903)

Bd367   Alègre, Jacques, 'EZ et l'école de la République', *Les Cahiers laïques*, 113 (1969), 113-40.

Bd368   Brombert, Victor, 'The Apostolate of Marc Froment', in *The Intellectual Hero: Studies in the French Novel, 1880-1955*, Philadelphia/New York: Lippincott, 1961; London: Faber, 1962, pp. 68-79.

Focuses on *Vérité*, but contains useful remarks on the themes and style of all of Z's later novels, seen against the background of the literature of ideas and ideology inaugurated by Bourget's *Le Disciple*; Z's enthusiasm for the 'intellectual' Marc Froment, a Republican schoolteacher, is incongruous because of Z's general scepticism towards intellectuals; his materialistic psychology also contributed to his lack of success in creating (as Bourget had done) a convincing drama of ideas.

Bd369   Paraf, Pierre, 'Z et l'instituteur', *Europe*, 372-3 (1960), 106-10.

Bd370   Ross, Peter, 'EZ, the Teachers and the Dreyfus Affair', *NFS*, XIV (Oct. 1975), 77-85.

A thorough account of Z's ideas on education in *Vérité*; the novel reflects his profound concern about ignorance: the Dreyfus Affair, which provides the framework of the novel, is seen as the supreme example of the consequences of mass ignorance, and the Catholic Church is attacked on the grounds that it promotes and thrives on ignorance.

See also Ba29; Bc71, 85, 144, 289, 290, 312, 313, 358, 375, 407.

Short Stories

Bd371   Austen-Smith, Jane, 'A Z Short Story: The Origins of a Political Mythology', *NFS*, XVIII (May 1979), 46-60.

A suggestive analysis of the political allegory, 'Aventures du grand Sidoine et du petit Médéric', which, it is argued, 'serves as a matrix for a number of images central to an understanding of the problematic nature of Z's ideological position as it receives expression in his mature novels.'

Bd372   Baguley, David, 'Les sources et la fortune des nouvelles de Z', *CN*, 32 (1966), 118-32.

Bd373   ——, 'Maupassant avant la lettre? A Study of a Z Short Story: "Les Coquillages de M. Chabre"' *NFS*, VI (Oct. 1967), 77-86.

Shows how Z's treatment of the cuckold theme differs from that of Maupassant in *Boule de suif*, published four years later.

Bd374 ——, 'Narcisse conteur: sur les contes de fées de Z', in Bb95, pp. 382-97.
Contains a penetrating thematic analysis of *La Fée amoureuse* and *Simplice*.

Bd375 Bellatore, André, 'Analyse d'un conte de Z: "Celle qui m'aime" ', *CN*, 47 (1974), 88-97.

Bd376 Christie, John, 'The Enigma of Z's "Madame Sourdis" ', *NFS*, V (May 1966), 13-28.

Bd377 Dédéyan, Charles, 'Z conteur et nouvelliste', in *Beiträge zur vergleichenden Literaturgeschichte. Festschrift für Kurt Wais*, ed. Johannes Hosle and Wolfgang Eitel, Tübingen: Niemeyer, 1972, pp. 253-63.

Bd378 Dumesnil, René, *La Publication des 'Soirées de Médan'*, Malfère, 1933, *passim*.
An account of the formation of the 'groupe de Médan' and the publication of *Les Soirées de Médan*.

Bd379 Gosse, Edmund, 'The Short Stories of Z', in *French Profiles*, London: Heinemann, 1905, pp. 129-52.

Bd380 Hemmings, F.W.J., 'Les sources d'inspiration de Z conteur', *CN*, 24-5 (1963), 29-44.
Concentrates on the *Contes à Ninon*; like John Lapp in Bb65, highlights themes which recur in Z's later work.

Bd381 Maupassant, Guy de, '*Les Soirées de Médan*. Comment ce livre a été fait', in *Chroniques, études, correspondance de Guy de Maupassant*, ed. René Dumesnil, Gründ, 1938, pp. 20-3.

Bd382 Ricatte, Robert, 'Z conteur', in Bb34, pp. 209-17.
A suggestive discussion of man/woman relationships in the later *contes*.

Bd383 Schoell, Konrad, 'Z: l'Inondation', in *Die französische Novelle*, ed. Wolfram Krömer, Düsseldorf: Bagel, 1976, pp. 163-70, 362-4.

Bd384 Weinberg, Henry H., 'Some Observations on the Early Development of Z's Style', *RR*, LXII (1971), 283-8.
Analyses the development of Z's style by comparing the final versions of *Nouveaux contes à Ninon* with early journalistic writings (1866-73) in

which they had their origin.

Bd385 ——, 'A Stylistic Comparison of Two Versions of Z's Short Story *Les Fraises*', *NCFS*, V (1976-7), 269-76.

See also Bb65; Bc90, 400; Bd137, 234, 278.

Be   Theatre, lyric dramas and theatrical adaptations of Z's works

Be1   Antoine, André, Refs in *Mes Souvenirs sur le Théâtre-Libre*, Fayard, 1921.

Be2   ——, 'EZ et le théâtre. L'interprétation et la mise en scène', *L'Information (politique)* (18.8.1924).
Cf. Bf2.

Be3   ——, Refs in *Mes Souvenirs sur le Théâtre Antoine et sur l'Odéon*, Grasset, 1928, esp. pp. 189-91.

Be4   Banville, Théodore de, 'Revue dramatique', *Le National* (14.7.1873 and 15.7.1873).
On *Thérèse Raquin*.

Be5   Barbier, Pierre, 'Le Naturalisme au théâtre', in Bb90, pp. 190-203.
Useful account of the fortune of Z's plays, his theatrical criticism and theories, and his influence.

Be6   Braescu, Ion, 'EZ, auteur dramatique', *Beiträge zur romanischen Philologie*, III (1964), 18-29.

Be7   Burns, C.A., '*L'Abbé Faujas*, une adaptation dramatique de *La Conquête de Plassans*', *CN*, 8-9 (1957), 378-81.

Be8   Cassaing, Jean-Claude, '*Les Parvenus* d'EZ. Un manuscrit inédit', *CN*, 52 (1978), 135-65.
A description of the plans for a play which throw new light on the thematic elaboration of the early novels of *Les Rougon-Macquart*.

Be9   Daudet, Alphonse, *Trente ans de Paris. A travers ma vie et mes livres*, Marpon & Flammarion, 1888, pp. 335-43.
An account of 'le dîner des auteurs sifflés' (gatherings of Z, Alphonse Daudet, Flaubert, Edmond de Goncourt and Turgenev).

Be10   Dietrich, Margaret, 'EZ', in *Europäische Dramaturgie im 19. Jahrhundert*, Graz/Cologne: Böhlaus, 1961, pp. 412-24.
On Z's conception of the Naturalist theatre and *Thérèse Raquin*.

Be11   Esslin, Martin, Refs in 'Naturalism in Context', *The Drama Review* (New York), XIII (Winter 1968), 67-76.
On the liberating influence of Z's theories.

Be12   Frichet-Rechou, Jacqueline, '*Nantas*: de la nouvelle au drame', *CN*,

41 (1971), 22-34.

Be13   ——, 'Le théâtre lyrique d'EZ', *CN*, 42 (1971), 171-80.

Be14   Guichard, Léon, 'Z et le drame lyrique', in *La Musique et les lettres en France au temps du wagnérisme*, P.U.F., 1963, pp. 213-16.

Be15   Guieu, Jean-Max, 'Z et le drame lyrique', in *Aux sources de la vérité du théâtre moderne. Actes du colloque de London (Canada)*, 1972, Minard (Lettres modernes), 1974, pp. 63-83.

Be16   Hemmings, F.W.J., 'EZ et le théâtre scandinave de son temps', *CN*, 29 (1965), 25-33.

Be17   Henderson, John A., Refs in *The First Avant-Garde (1887-1894): Sources of the Modern French Theatre*, London: Harrap, 1971 (esp. pp. 27-30).

Be18   Heriot, Angus, 'EZ as Librettist', *Opera* (London), XI (1960), 595-9.

Be19   Kanes, Martin, 'Z and Busnach: The Temptation of the Stage', *PMLA*, LXXVII (1962), 109-15.
An account of the nature of Z's theatrical collaboration with William Busnach, observations on the relationship between Z *romancier* and Z *dramaturge*, and speculative remarks on the reasons for Z's attraction to the stage.

Be20   ——, 'Z, *Germinal* et la censure dramatique', *CN*, 29 (1965), 35-42.
Sees Z's three-year campaign against official censorship of his play as a conscious struggle against the vestiges of Imperial tyranny and a curious prefiguration of his disinterested struggle for justice in the Dreyfus Affair.

Be21   Lefrançois, Philippe, 'L'adaptation de *L'Assommoir* et de *Nana* à la scène', *Le Miroir de l'histoire*, 70 (1955), 597-605.

Be22   Lemaitre, Jules, 'EZ. Matinée du Vaudeville: reprise de *Thérèse Raquin*, drame en quatre actes', in *Impressions de théâtre*, VII, Lecène & Oudin, 1894, pp. 183-9.

Be23   Lote, Georges, 'Les réformateurs du théâtre à la fin du XIXe siècle, I: La dramaturgie d'EZ', *Revue de la Méditerranée* (Algiers), III (1946), 152-70.

Be24   Melcher, Edith, Refs in *Stage Realism in France. Between Diderot and Antoine*, New York: Russell & Russell, 1976.

Be25   Mitterand, Henri, '*Thérèse Raquin* au théâtre', *RSH*, 104 (1961), 489-516.

Be26 Pagès, Alain, 'La tabatière à musique (sur *Les Mystères de Marseille* au théâtre)', in Bb95, pp. 323-34.

Be27 Pryme, Eileen E., 'Z's Plays in England, 1870-1900', *FS*, XIII (1959), 28-38.

Be28 Robichez, Jacques, Refs in *Le Symbolisme au théâtre. Lugné-Poe et les débuts de L'Oeuvre*, L'Arche, 1957 (esp. pp. 28-33).

Be29 Sanders, James B., 'Antoine, Z et le théâtre', *CN*, 42 (1971), 51-60 (see also 71-6, 109-10).

Be30 ——, 'Antoine et Z', *CN*, 50 (1976), 9-18.

Be31 ——, 'Busnach, Z et le drame de *l'Assommoir*', *CN*, 52 (1978), 109-2

Be32 Sarcey, Francisque, *Quarante ans de théâtre (feuilletons dramatiques,* VII, Bibliothèque des Annales politiques et littéraires, 1902, pp. 1-84 Contains reviews of *Renée, L'Assommoir, Pot-Bouille* and *Le Ventre de Paris*.

Be33 Sarthou, Jacques, 'Le naturalisme au théâtre ... en 1956', *CN*, 5 (1956), 240-3.
On *Les Héritiers Rabourdin*.

Be34 Souriau, Etienne, 'Sur une nouvelle formule de réalisme au théâtre', *Revue d'esthétique*, XXVII (1974), 107-15.

Be35 Treusch-Dieter, Gerbug, 'Was hat von Z verstanden? Ueberlegungen zur Dramatisierung und Aufführung von *Germinal* am Frankfurter TAT', *Theater heute*, XV (Oct. 1974), 12-16.

Be36 Whiting, George W., '*Volpone, Herr von Fuchs*, and *Les Héritiers Rabourdin*', *PMLA*, XLVI (1931), 605-7.

See also Bb21, 86.

Bf   Critical Works and the Naturalist Aesthetic

Bf1   Adhémar, Jean and Hélène, 'Le critique d'art', in Bb124, pp. 53-70.

Bf2   Antoine, 'EZ et le théâtre. La doctrine', *L'Information (politique)* (11.8.1924).
Cf. Be2.

Bf3   Auriant, L., 'Duranty et Z (lettres inédites)', *La Nef*, 20 (July 1946), 43-58.

Bf4   Bahr, Hermann, 'Z', in *Die Überwindung des Naturalismus*, Dresden/ Leipzig: Pierson, 1891, pp. 173-84.
A discussion of *La Bête humaine* in the context of Z's aesthetic: argues that Z's theories are absurdly irrelevant to his achievement of powerful imaginative effects.

Bf5   Baschet, Robert, 'La critique d'art d'EZ (1866-1896)', *RDM* (1.12.1966), 360-70.

Bf6   Becker, Colette, 'Aux sources du naturalisme zolien (1860-1865)', in Bb84, pp. 13-33.

Bf7   ——, 'EZ: 1862-1867. Elaboration d'une esthétique moderne', *Romantisme*, 21-2 (1978), 117-23.

Bf8   Becker, George J., Refs in 'Modern Realism as a Literary Movement', in George J. Becker, ed., *Documents of Modern Literary Realism*, Princeton U.P., 1963, pp. 3-38.

Bf9   Bellos, David, 'The Impact of EZ', in *Balzac Criticism in France, 1850-1900: The Making of a Reputation*, Oxford: Clarendon Press, 1976, pp. 98-142.

Bf10   Bevernis, Christa, 'Balzac et Z: sur quelques aspects de leurs théories esthétiques', in Bb34, pp. 282-6.

Bf11   Bourget, Paul, 'Le Naturalisme au théâtre', *Le Parlement* (28.2.1881); repr. in *Etudes et portraits*, I, Lemerre, 1889, pp. 340-9.
A review of *Le Naturalisme au théâtre* (1881).

Bf12   Braudy, Leo, 'Z on Film: The Ambiguities of Naturalism', in Bb119, pp. 68-88.
Focuses on the pervasive motif of the observer in Z's novels. Shows how many novels contain internal subversions or parodies of the 'scientific' method of

detached observation, reflecting an obsession with the nature of observation and a tension between involvement and detachment which has a strong affinity with the essential aesthetic and epistemological nature of the cinema; contains a survey of screen adaptations of Z's novels (most of these concentrate on naturalistic reconstruction, but the better ones, like Jean Renoir's 1926 version of *Nana*, bring out more clearly than in the novels Z's ambiguous attitude towards Naturalism) and a filmography; cf. Bc152, 206, 232, 330, 344; Bd19? 326.

Bf13   Brookner, Anita, 'Z', in *The Genius of the Future. Studies in French Art Criticism*, London: Phaidon, 1971, pp. 89-117.
A readable and incisive general account of Z's achievement as an art critic, including remarks on the relationship between his art criticism and his fiction.

Bf14   Brunius, Teddy, 'Edouard Manet, EZ, and Naturalism', in *Mutual Aid in the Arts from the Second Empire to Fin de Siècle*, Uppsala: Almqvist & Wicksell, 1972, pp. 59-89.

Bf15   Butler, R., 'Z Between Taine and Sainte-Beuve 1863-1869', *MLR*, LXIX (1974), 279-89.
A study in Z's reactions to Taine's critical method in articles and letters written between 1864 and 1869 which challenges the view that Z was profoundly influenced by Taine at this period: these writings reveal a growing hostility to what Z saw as the dogmatic inflexibility of Taine's method; Z's insistence on the primacy of individuality in artistic creation found support in the critical approach of Sainte-Beuve, who was similarly opposed to Taine, whose impact on Z emerges as short-lived and limited.

Bf16   ——, 'Z's Art Criticism (1865-1868)', *FMLS*, X (1974), 334-47.
The confusions and inconsistencies of the art criticism produced from 1865 to 1868 reflect a transitional phase in which Z was attempting to work out 'a coherent aesthetic in which poetry and realism would be blended'; the 1868 *Salon* is disappointingly barren compared with the fire and originality of the 1866 *Salon*, but it marks the end of a crisis in Z's aesthetic development.

Bf17   Charensol, Georges, 'Z et les peintres', in Bb90, pp. 183-9.

Bf18   Chiari, Joseph, 'Realism and Naturalism', in *The Aesthetics of Modernism*, London: Vision Press, 1970, pp. 49-95 (see esp. pp. 75-80).

Bf19   Courthion, Pierre, 'Petite note sur Z critique d'art', in Bb34, pp. 252-5.
Brief general remarks.

Bf20   Daix, Pierre, 'Z contre la révolution dans la peinture', in *L'Aveugle-ment devant la peinture*, Gallimard, 1971, pp. 117-98; see also pp. 205-7, 213-19.

A structuralist view of Z's art criticism and of *L'Oeuvre*. Discusses Z's failure to understand 'modernity' in painting with a view to showing that 'la naissance de la peinture moderne ne met pas en cause que la lecture de la peinture, mais des changements dans l'idéologie, dans les systèmes de signification'.

Bf21   David-Sauvageot, A., Refs in *Le Réalisme et le naturalisme dans la littérature et dans l'art*, Calmann Lévy, 1890. /

Bf22   Dort, Bernard, 'Un "nouveau" critique: EZ', in *Théâtre réel. Essais de critique, 1967-1970*, Seuil, 1971, pp. 31-43.

Stresses Z's importance (reflected in his critical and theoretical writings rather than his plays) as a forerunner of the modern theatre: 'Z est le premier témoin d'une rupture décisive dans l'exercice du théâtre.'

Bf23   Ebin, Ima N., 'Manet et Z', *Gazette des Beaux-Arts*, XXVII (1945), 357-78.

Bf24   Ehrard, Antoinette, 'Z et Courbet', in Bb34, pp. 241-51.

Bf25   Farrell, James T., Refs in 'Some Observations on Naturalism, So Called, in Fiction', *Antioch Review* (Yellow Springs, Ohio), X (1950), 247-64.

A vigorous defence of Naturalism as a literary tendency which has 'encouraged a spirit of truth and free inquiry'.

Bf26   Furst, Lilian R., 'Z's Art Criticism', in *French 19th Century Painting and Literature, with Special Reference to the Relevance of Literary Subject-matter to French Painting*, ed. U. Finke, Manchester U.P., 1972, pp. 164-81.

An excellent discussion of Z and Impressionism; Z was attracted to the Impressionists because he saw in them the artistic equivalent of Naturalism (emphasis on modernity, etc.), and his later disillusion, reflected in his *Salon de 1896*, was caused by what he saw as their failure to live up to their aims.

Bf27   ——, and Peter N. Skrine, *Naturalism* (The Critical Idiom, 18), London: Methuen, 1971.

Bf28   Gahide, Françoise, '*Le Naturalisme au théâtre* d'EZ ... ou les origines de la crise au théâtre', *Théâtre populaire*, 31 (1958), 1-11.

Bf29   Gauthier, E. Paul, 'Z on Naturalism in Art and History', *MLN*, LXX (1955), 514-17.

A quarrel with Stasyulevitch, editor of *Vestnik Evropy*, over Z's use of the word 'Naturalism' in his articles for the Russian periodical.

Bf30   Gosse, Edmund, 'The Limits of Realism in Fiction', in *Questions at Issue*, London: Heinemann, 1893, pp. 137-54; repr. in George J. Becker, ed., *Documents of Modern Literary Realism*, Princeton U.P., 1963, pp. 383-93.

Bf31   Guedj, Aimé, 'Diderot et Z. Essai de redéfinition du naturalisme', in Bb34, pp. 287-324.
A richly suggestive study of the vision and methods of Naturalism.

Bf32   ——, Refs in 'Le naturalisme avant Z. La littérature et la science sous le Second Empire', in Bb94, pp. 567-80.

Bf33   Hamilton, George H., 'Manet and Z, 1866-1867', in *Manet and his Critics*, New Haven: Yale U.P., 1954, pp. 81-111.

Bf34   Hart, Heinrich and Julius, 'Für und gegen Z', *Kritische Waffengänge* (Leipzig), 2 (1882), 47-55; repr. in George J. Becker, ed., *Documents of Modern Literary Realism*, Princeton U.P., 1963, pp. 251-60.
An important document in the literary history of Germany; the example of Z's Naturalism is seen to show the possibility of the revitalization of German literature by the erosion of prevailing conventions; cf. Bf44.

Bf35   Hatzfeld, Helmut A., Refs in 'Discussion sur le naturalisme français', *Studies in Philology*, XXXIX (1942), 696-726.
A broad schematic survey of the theoretical bases, aesthetic principles, philosophical and social vision, characteristic themes and stylistic features of Naturalism.

Bf36   Hemmings, F.W.J., 'The Origin of the Terms *Naturalisme, Naturaliste*', *FS*, VIII (1954), 109-21.
It was probably Z's reading of Taine (the Balzac essay of 1858) which encouraged him to incorporate the term 'naturaliste' into his critical vocabulary; Z's own claim that the word 'naturalisme' is found in Montaigne is groundless, but there is more substance in his assertion that the term was already common currency in Russia, for the critic Belinsky had used it freely in the 1840s.

Bf37   ——, 'Z faux-frère de Manet? ou les citations dangereuses', *CN*, 8-9 (1957), 386-9.
Shows how deliberate quotation out of context of an 1879 article in *Vestnik Evropy* on the Impressionists led to false accounts of Z's perfidy towards Manet; cf. Bf38.

Bf38   ——, 'Z, Manet, and the Impressionists (1875-80)', *PMLA*, LXXIII (1958), 407-17.
Shows that Z's articles in *Vestnik Evropy* prove him to have been a far more prolific writer on the contemporary art scene than had been supposed and that, despite the common belief that his support for the Impressionists subsided at the end of the sixties, he retained much of his earlier enthusiasm for the group; cf. Bf37.

Bf39   ——, 'Z and *L'Education sentimentale*', *RR*, L (1959), 35-40.
Compares Z's differing assessments of the novel, written in 1869 and 1879: in the first article he writes perceptively (and with a degree of self-identification) of the duality of Flaubert's artistic temperament (the 'realist' and 'poet'); while in the second he speaks of Flaubert only as the 'realist' novelist *par excellence*. The change in the aesthetic criteria Z applied in these articles implies that in 1879 he was less interested in criticism than in propaganda for Naturalism; and a further conclusion is that Z is a more acute literary critic than is generally thought and that his more perceptive and richer criticism is to be found in the press-articles written during his earlier, less doctrinaire period.

Bf40   ——, 'La critique d'un créateur: Z et Malot', *RHLF*, LXVII (1967), 55-67.
Z's reviews of the novels of Hector Malot reveal the possibility of a minor influence.

Bf41   ——, '*Le Candidat* de Flaubert dans la critique d'EZ', *RSH*, 131 (1968), 465-75.
On four brief but sympathetic articles in *Le Sémaphore de Marseille* concerning Flaubert's unsuccessful play.

Bf42   ——, 'EZ, critique d'art', in EZ, *Salons*, ed. F.W.J. Hemmings and Robert J. Niess, Geneva: Droz; Paris: Minard, 1959, pp. 9-42.
An excellent account of the development of Z's attitude to art; describes the background to each article included in this valuable collection of 11 articles (which range over 30 years — from the *Salon* of 1866 to that of 1896).

Bf43   Hérain, François de, 'EZ', in *Les Grands Ecrivains critiques d'art*, Mercure de France, 1943, pp. 117-25.

Bf44   Holz, Arno, 'Z als Theoretiker', in *Die Kunst. Ihr Wesen und ihre Gesetze*, Berlin: Issleib, 1891, pp. 68-83; repr. in *Das Werk von Arno Holz*, X, Berlin: Nachfolger, 1925, pp. 51-61.
Cf. Bf34.

Bf45   Kuczynski, Jürgen, 'Z — Wissenschaft und Kunst', in *Gestalten und Werke*, II, Berlin/Weimar: Aufbau, 1971, pp. 389-417.

Bf46   Lalo, Charles, 'Taine et Z. L'esthétique naturaliste et l'esthétique réaliste', *Revue bleue*, n.s., XLIX (1911), 214-18, 236-42.

Bf47   Lanson, Gustave, 'La littérature et la science', *Revue bleue*, L (1892), 385-91, 433-40.

Bf48   Lapp, John C., 'Taine et Z: autour d'une correspondance', *RSH*, 87 (1957), 319-26.
Six letters from Taine, written between 1866 and 1875, which reveal his significant influence on Z's conception of *Les Rougon-Macquart*.

Bf49   Lethève, Jacques, Refs in *Impressionnistes et symbolistes devant la presse*, Armand Colin, 1959 (esp. pp. 35-51, 113-20).

Bf50   Lindsay, Jack, 'Note sur Z et sa méthode', in Bb33, pp. 201-5.
Z as a precursor of socialist realism.

Bf51   Lote, Georges, 'La doctrine et la méthode naturalistes d'après EZ', *Zeitschrift für französische Sprache und Literatur*, LI (1928), 193-22 389-418.

Bf52   Markiewicz, Henryk, 'Le naturalisme dans les recherches littéraires et dans l'esthétique du XXe siècle', *RLC*, XLVII (1973), 256-72.
Argues that 'le naturalisme en tant que phénomène littéraire à l'échelle mondiale reste toujours mal connu' and advocates that Naturalism be viewed in a broad European context rather than as a narrow literary tradition springing from Z; constitutes a useful bibliographical survey.

Bf53   Martino, Pierre, 'Vers le naturalisme. Les premiers romans scientifiques de Z (1865-1870)', in *Le Roman réaliste sous le second Empire*, Hachette, 1913, pp. 255-86.

Bf54   Matthews, J.H., 'Note sur la méthode de Z (documents inédits)', *RSH*, 83 (1956), 337-46.
Despite Z's disavowal in *Le Roman expérimental* of any artistic manipulation of his material, an examination of the *dossiers* and texts of *Les Rougon-Macquart* immediately reveals his subjective vision and clear artistic intentions.

Bf55   Mitterand, Henri, 'La formation littéraire d'EZ: la naissance du naturalisme', *CN*, 24-5 (1963), 21-3.
Cursory remarks on the influences Z underwent, and the development of his literary sensibility, during the ten formative years which preceded the publication of *Thérèse Raquin* (1867).

Bf56   Mouchard, Claude, 'Naturalisme et anthropologie (à partir du *Docteur Pascal*)', in Bb84, pp. 391-406.

Bf57   Müller, Hans-Joachim, *Der Roman des Realismus-Naturalismus in Frankreich. Eine erkenntnistheoretische Studie*, Wiesbaden: Athenaion, 1977 (esp. pp. 22-38).

Bf58   Niess, Robert J., 'EZ and Impressionism in Painting', *American Society of Legion of Honor Magazine*, XXXIX (1968), 87-101.

Bf59   Nochlin, Linda, Refs in *Realism*, Harmondsworth: Penguin Books, 1971.

Bf60   Pagès, Alain, 'En partant de la théorie du roman expérimental', *CN*, 47 (1974), 70-87.
Argues that Z's stated theories, contrary to general assumptions, do provide useful conceptual tools for the analysis of his fiction; focuses on characterization and the use of *le style indirect libre* (most examples are taken from *Germinal*).

Bf61   Pardo Bazán, Emilia, Refs in *La cuestión palpitante*, Madrid: Imprenta central a cargo de V. Saíz, 1883; French tr.: *Le Naturalisme*, tr. Albert Savine, Giraud, 1886; repr. (with a new preface and a letter from Z) in *Obras completas*, I, Madrid: Pérez Dubrull, 1891.
A defence of Naturalism. Cf. Bc100.

Bf62   Perruchot, Henri, 'Z et les impressionnistes', *La Pensée française*, XVIII (March 1959), 22-7.

Bf63   Picon, Gaëtan, 'Z's Painters', in Bb119, pp. 126-42; repr. in J.-P. Bouillon, ed., *Le Bon Combat. De Courbet aux Impressionnistes* (Coll. Savoir), Hermann, 1974, pp. 7-22.
Outlines the attitudes that informed Z's early enthusiasm for the Impressionists and argues that the reasons for the progressive waning of this enthusiasm reveals certain failures in his perception of Impressionism, of the 'artistic movement', and also of his own art, which is inextricably related to the Impressionist aesthetic.

Bf64   Raimond, Michel, 'La crise du roman naturaliste' and 'Au lendemain du naturalisme', in *La Crise du roman. Des lendemains du naturalisme aux années vingt*, José Corti, 1966, pp. 25-43, 299-311.

Bf65   Rees, Garnet, 'The Influence of Science on the Structure of the Novel (Balzac, Flaubert, Z)', in *Literature and Science. International Federation for Modern Languages and Literatures: Proceedings of the Sixth Triennial Congress*, Oxford: Blackwell, 1955, pp. 255-61.

With Balzac and Flaubert the techniques of the novel were greatly advanced by the influence of science, while the virtues of Z's work lie outside the author's scientific pretensions.

Bf66   Reizov, B., 'L'esthétique de Z', in Bb34, pp. 372-85.

Bf67   Rheims, Maurice, 'EZ et la curiosité', *CN*, 46 (1973), 121-9.
On Z's achievement as an art critic.

Bf68   Ripoll, Roger, 'Z et le modèle positiviste', *Romantisme*, 21-2 (1978), 125-35.
On the nature and evolution of Z's conception of positivism.

Bf69   Robert, Guy, 'Z et le classicisme', *RSH*, 49 (1948), 1-24; 50 (1948), 126-53.
Based on the critical writings of 1875-80; outlines Z's debt to the classical tradition and his ambivalent attitude towards it; cf. Bc394.

Bf70   Rostand, Jean, 'Z et la science', in Bb90, pp. 153-7.

Bf71   ——, 'L'oeuvre de Z et la pensée scientifique', in Bb34, pp. 360-9.

Bf72   Schalk, Fritz, 'Zur Romantheorie und Praxis von Z', in *Beiträge zur Theorie der Künste im 19. Jahrhundert*, I, Frankfurt am Main: Klostemann, 1971, pp. 337-51.

Bf73   Scherer, Edmond, 'Le manifeste du roman naturaliste' and 'EZ', in *Etudes sur la littérature contemporaine*, VII, Calmann Lévy, 1882, pp. 165-76, 176-89.

Bf74   Schober, Rita, 'Zs ästhetische Auseinandersetzung mit Balzac', in *Von der wirklichen Welt in der Dichtung. Aufsätze zur Theorie und Praxis des Realismus in der französischen Literatur*, Berlin/Weimar: Aufbau, 1970, pp. 185-213; repr. in *Der französische Roman im 19. Jahrhundert*, ed. Winfried Engler, Darmstadt: Wissenschaftliche Buchgesellschaft, 1976, pp. 427-72.

Bf75   Seznec, Jean, 'Renan, Z, et les visions de Jeanne d'Arc', in *Balzac and the Nineteenth Century. Studies in French Literature presented to Herbert J. Hunt*, ed. D.G. Charlton, J. Gaudon and A.R. Pugh, Leicester U.P., 1972, pp. 365-75.
On the contrasting attitudes of Z and Renan towards religious art.

Bf76   Shiff, Richard, 'The End of Impressionism: A Study in Theories of Artistic Expression', *Art Quarterly*, n.s., I (1978), 338-78 (pp. 357-60

An important article focusing on the relation between Impressionist and Symbolist conceptions of artistic expression.

Bf77 Souffrin, Eileen, 'Banville et Z, avec des lettres inédites', *CN*, 24-5 (1963), 57-66.

Bf78 Suwala, Halina, 'Première campagne critique de Z (1865-1866)', in Bb95, pp. 310-22.

Bf79 Taslitzky, Boris, 'Notes sur la critique d'art (Malraux, Z, Aragon)', *La Nouvelle Critique*, 39 (1952), 58-76 (pp. 65-9).
Attacks misinterpretations of Z's article 'Adieu d'un critique d'art', arguing that 'il n'y eut jamais de différend entre Z et les Impressionnistes, mais entre Z et la queue de l'Impressionnisme'.

Bf80 Trudgian, Helen, 'Claude Bernard and the "Groupe de Médan"', in *Literature and Science. International Federation for Modern Languages and Literatures: Proceedings of the Sixth Triennial Congress*, Oxford: Blackwell, 1955, pp. 273-6.

Bf81 Varloot, Jean, 'Z vivant: I. Le procès du naturalisme', *La Pensée*, n.s., 44 (1952), 111-21.

Bf82 ——, 'Z vivant: II. Le réalisme de Z', *La Pensée*, n.s., 46 (1953), 17-28.
A Marxist view.

Bf83 Vicaire, Gabriel, 'L'esthétique d'EZ', *RDM*, n.s., XXI (1924), 810-31.

Bf84 Walter, Rodolphe, 'Critique d'art et vérité: EZ en 1868', *Gazette des Beaux-Arts*, LXXIII (1969), 225-34.
Examines Z's comments, in *Mon Salon* (1868), on four paintings by Corot, Monet, Renoir and Manet with a view to establishing that the coincidence between his aesthetics and his moral philosophy may be summed up in the word 'truth'.

Bf85 Weinberg, Henry H., 'Z: Some Early Critical Concepts', *MLQ*, XXVIII (1967), 207-12.
Some of Z's earliest journalistic work, published in *La Tribune* between 1868 and 1870, helps to elucidate his views on truth, modernism, and the role of science in literature, and thus helps to contribute to our knowledge of the crucial early development of his literary doctrine.

Bf86 Weiss, J.-J., 'Réalisme et naturalisme', in *Le Théâtre et les moeurs*, Calmann Lévy, 1889, pp. 237-54.

Bf87   Wellek, René, 'EZ (1840-1902)', in *A History of Modern Criticism: 1750-1950*, IV. *The Later Nineteenth Century*, New Haven: Yale U.P., 1965, pp. 14-22.

See also Bb27, 30, 42, 74, 77, 107; Bc42, 56, 60, 100, 101, 140, 175, 177, 178, 193, 209, 219, 256, 258, 295, 349, 363, 380; Bd27, 104, 136, 248, 259; Be5; Bg23.

Articles

Bg Journalism

Bg1 Bakker, B.H. 'Z, Alexis et l'affaire *Henri IV*', *CN*, 42 (1971), 41-50.
A demonstration of Z's polemical flair as a journalist.

Bg2 Bellanger, Claude, 'Il y a cent ans, EZ faisait à Lille ses débuts dans la presse. Une correspondance inédite', *CN*, 26 (1964), 5-44.
Correspondence between Z and a journalist named Géry-Legrand; useful insights into Z's activities during the period 1863-5.

Bg3 Boulouis, Jean, '*La République en marche* ou les débuts de la Troisième vus par EZ', *Politique*, n.s., 6 (1959), 182-95.

Bg4 Chemel, Henri, 'Z collaborateur du *Sémaphore* de Marseille (1871-1877)', *CN*, 14 (1960), 555-67; 18 (1961), 71-9.

Bg5 De Amicis, Edmondo, 'EZ polemista', in *Ritratti letterari*, Milan: Treves, 1881, pp. 51-106.
On *Une Campagne*.

Bg6 Delas, Daniel, 'Z et la démocratie parlementaire 1871-1881', in Bb34, pp. 27-36.
An account of the growing anti-parliamentarianism discernible in the articles Z wrote for *La Cloche* and *Le Figaro*.

Bg7 Dezalay, Auguste, 'Cent ans après. Un journaliste bien parisien: EZ portraitiste', *CN*, 34 (1967), 114-23.
An analysis of the attitudes displayed by Z in a series of nine literary portraits entitled *Marbres et plâtres* (published in *Le Figaro* in 1866-7).

Bg8 Duncan, Phillip, A., 'The Fortunes of Z's *Parizskie Pis'ma* in Russia', *Slavic and East European Journal*, XVII (1959), 107-21.
On the impact made on 'progressive' thinking in Russia by the *Lettres de Paris* Z wrote for *Vestnik Evropy* from 1875 to 1880.

Bg9 Dupuy, Aimé, 'EZ, chroniqueur parlementaire à Bordeaux et à Versailles', in *1870-1871. La Guerre, la Commune et la presse*, Armand Colin, 1959, pp. 151-66.

Bg10 Hemmings, F.W.J., 'Z on the Staff of *Le Gaulois*', *MLR*, L (1955), 25-9.

Bg11 ——, 'Z, *Le Bien public* and *Le Voltaire*', *RR*, XLVII (1956), 103-16.

Bg12 ——, 'Z's Apprenticeship to Journalism (1865-70)', *PMLA*, LXXI (1956), 340-54.

Bg13   Kanes, Martin, 'Introduction', in *L'Atelier de Z. Textes de journaux 1865-1870*, ed. Kanes, Geneva: Droz, 1963, pp. 1-21.
Contains some perceptive observations on the ways in which Z's early journalism may be seen as a literary workshop in which the author forged a personal style.

Bg14   ——, 'Z, Pelletan and *La Tribune*', *PMLA*, LXXIX (1964), 473-83.

Bg15   Kayser, Jacques, 'Z journaliste', *CN*, 3 (1955), 106-15.
A superficial and fragmentary introduction.

Bg16   Manevy, Raymond, 'A l'occasion du cinquantenaire de la mort de l'auteur de "J'accuse". EZ journaliste', *Etudes de presse*, III (1952), 36-45.

Bg17   Mitterand, Henri, 'EZ et *le Rappel*', *CN*, 15 (1960), 589-604.

Bg18   ——, ed., 'La correspondance (inédite) entre EZ et Michel Stassulevitch, directeur du *Messager de l'Europe* (1875-1881)', *CN*, 22 (1962) 255-79.
Shows that the monthly articles Z wrote for *Vestnik Evropy*, a St Petersburg literary review, constitute a rich source of information on his literary opinions and his views on aspects of French social, political and cultural life; cf. Bb80 (pp. 185-202); Bg19, 25.

Bg19   Montreynaud, Florence, ed., 'La correspondance entre Z et Stassioule vitch [*sic*], directeur du *Messager de l'Europe* (deuxième partie)', *CN*, 47 (1974), 1-39.
Cf. Bb80 (pp. 185-202); Bg18, 25.

Bg20   Ripoll, Roger, 'Quelques articles retrouvés de *La Marseillaise*', *CN*, 34 (1967), 148-64.

Bg21   ——, 'Z juge de Victor Hugo (1871-1877)', *CN*, 46 (1973), 182-204.
An account of Z's sustained polemic during the early years of the Third Republic against the literary and political views of Hugo.

Bg22   ——, ed., 'Z collaborateur de *La Vraie République*', *CN*, 51 (1977), 120-40.
Detective work on Z's activities as a journalist in Marseilles in November 1870 and suggestions as to which unsigned articles might be his.

Bg23   Tancock, Leonard W., 'Some Early Critical Work of EZ: *Livres d'aujourd'hui et de demain* (1886)', *MLR*, XLII (1947), 43-57.

Bg24   Thomas, Marcel, 'Le journaliste politique', in Bb124, pp. 71-85.

Bg25   Triomphe, Jean, 'Z collaborateur du *Messager de l'Europe*', *RLC*,
        XVII (1937), 754-65.
        On Z's five-year collaboration with the St Petersburg monthly *Vestnik Evropy*;
        cf. Bb80 (pp. 185-202); Bg18, 19.

Bg26   Weinberg, Henry H., 'Ironie et idéologie: Z à la naissance de la
        troisième République', *CN*, 42 (1971), 61-70.
        On the parliamentary reports Z contributed to *La Cloche* in 1871.

Bg27   ——, 'Z and the Paris Commune: The *La Cloche* Chronicles', *NCFS*,
        VIII (1979-80), 76-86.
        Again brings out Z's lack of sympathy for the Commune. Cf. Bc169, 331.

See also Bb23, 38, 80, 81, 97; Bc163, 166, 169, 331; Bd384.

Bh   The Dreyfus Affair

Bh1   Barrès, Maurice, *Scènes et doctrines du nationalisme*, Juven, 1902,
         pp. 40-3; repr. as 'Z' in *L'Oeuvre de Maurice Barrès*, ed. Philippe
         Barrès, V, Club de l'Honnête Homme, 1966, pp. 52-4.
         '... EZ pense tout naturellement en Vénitien déraciné. Les esprits perspicaces
         ont toujours senti ce qu'il y a d'étranger, voire d'anti-français, dans le talent
         de Z.'

Bh2   Bettinson, C.D., and L.J. Newton, 'EZ: Idealist in Politics', *Modern
         Languages*, LIV (1973), 119-25.

Bh3   Boussel, Patrice, 'Les Affaires Esterhazy, Z, Picquart ... (et Dreyfus)',
         in *L'Affaire Dreyfus et la presse* (Coll. kiosque), Armand Colin, 1960
         pp. 155-79.

Bh4   Chapman, Guy, 'The Intervention of Z', in *The Dreyfus Trials*, Lon-
         don: Batsford, 1972, pp. 125-43; London: Paladin, 1974, pp. 129-46

Bh5   Cogny, Pierre, 'La rhétorique de la vérité dans *J'accuse*', *CN*, 46 (197
         130-8.
         A study of Z's rhetorical style in *J'accuse*.

Bh6   Daspre, André, 'Z et les intellectuels dans l'Affaire Dreyfus', in Bb34,
         pp. 41-6.
         Dreyfusisme seen as the birth of the conception of the intellectual.

Bh7   Delhorbe, Cécile, 'EZ', in *L'Affaire Dreyfus et les écrivains français*,
         Attinger, 1932, pp. 45-80.
         Z's romantic *dreyfusisme* seen in the context of the quasi-religious nature of
         his later works.

Bh8   Dezalay, Auguste, 'La défense des innocents et le respect de la loi.
         Z et l'Affaire Dreyfus', *Journalisme*, 37 (1971), 35-9.
         J'accuse as the apotheosis of Z's career as a combative and truth-seeking
         journalist.

Bh9   Drumont, Edouard, 'EZ', in *Les Tréteaux du succès. Figures de
         bronze ou statues de neige*, Flammarion, 1900, pp. 165-95.
         Vituperative.

Bh10   Furst, Lilian R., 'Z's Motivation in the Dreyfus Affair', *Niv Hamid-
         rashia* (Tel Aviv), XI (1974), 134-43.

Bh11   Guillemin, Henri, 'Une ignominie exemplaire: Judet contre Z (1898)'

and 'Z et l'Affaire Dreyfus', in *Eclaircissements*, Gallimard, 1961, pp. 251-64, 265-85.
The first item concerns Ernest Judet's attacks on Z in *Le Petit Journal*.

Bh12 ——, 'L'Affaire', in Bb124, pp. 231-51.

Bh13 Hemmings, F.W.J., 'The Explosion of Truth', in *Culture and Society in France 1848-1898. Dissidents and Philistines*, London: Batsford, 1971, pp. 254-63.

Bh14 Johnson, Douglas, Refs in *France and the Dreyfus Affair*, London: Blandford, 1966.

Bh15 Jourdain, Francis, 'EZ devant les cannibales', in Bb33, pp. 7-26.

Bh16 Kayser, Jacques, 'J'accuse!' and 'Le procès Z', in *L'Affaire Dreyfus*, Gallimard, 1946, pp. 112-32, 133-63.

Bh17 ——, ' "J'accuse !" ', *Europe*, 25 (1948), 11-21.

Bh18 ——, 'EZ et l'opinion publique', *La Nef*, 49 (1948), 47-58; 50 (1949), 23-37.
A selection from the vast correspondence received by Z during the Dreyfus Affair.

Bh19 ——, 'Z et l'affaire Dreyfus', in Bb90, pp. 171-5.

Bh20 Mendès-France, Pierre, 'Le pélerinage de Médan 1956: discours de M. Pierre Mendès-France', *CN*, 6 (1956), 265-71; repr. in *La Vérité guidait leurs pas*, Gallimard, 1976, pp. 71-82.

Bh21 Miquel, Pierre, *L'Affaire Dreyfus* (Coll. 'Que sais-je? '), P.U.F., 1959, pp. 43-71.

Bh22 ——, 'Z et l'Affaire Dreyfus', *CN*, 16 (1960), 634-40.

Bh23 Psichari, Henriette, Refs in 'Silhouettes dreyfusardes', in *Des jours et des hommes (1890-1961)*, Grasset, 1962, pp. 31-55.

Bh24 Thalheimer, Siegfried, 'Anatole France und EZ' and 'Zs Prozess', in *Macht und Gerechtigkeit. Ein Beitrag zur Geschichte des Falles Dreyfus*, Munich: Beck'sche, 1958, pp. 265-93, 294-375.

Bh25 Thomas, Marcel, 'EZ et "L'Affaire" ', *Aesculape*, n.s., XXXIII (1952), 212-16.

Bh26 ——, Refs in *L'Affaire sans Dreyfus*, Fayard, 1961; Geneva: Edito-

service, 1971.
A most scrupulous study.

Bh27 Wilson, Nelly, Refs in *Bernard Lazare: Antisemitism and the Problem of Jewish Identity in Late Nineteenth-century France*, CUP, 1978.
Bernard Lazare was a leading *dreyfusard*; his brochure 'Une erreur judiciaire' anticipated Z's 'J'accuse' by three years.

Bh28 Wood, John S., 'La correspondance Joseph Reinach-EZ', *CN*, 51 (1977), 188-239.

Bh29 Zévaès, Alexandre, 'EZ en cour d'assises: le procès de "J'accuse"', in Bb90, pp. 140-8.

See also Bb122; Bc98, 143, 246; Bd370.

INDEX OF AUTHORS' NAMES

Abastado, Claude, Bb1

Adam, Jean-Michel, Bd141

Adam, Paul, Bc1

Adhémar, Hélène, Bf1

Adhémar, Jean, Bc2, 3; Bf1

Agulhon, M., Bd127

Ähnebrink, Lars, Bb2; Bc4

Alas, Leopoldo: see Clarín

Albalat, Antoine, Bc5

Albérès, R.-M., Bd14

Alcorn, Clayton R., Jr, Bc6, 7; Bd73, 227

Alègre, Jacques, Bd367

Alexis, Paul, Bb3

Allard, Jacques, Bb4

Antoine, André, Be1-3; Bf2

Aragon, Louis, Bc8

Armstrong, Judith, Bc9

Arrighi, Paul, Bc10, 11; Bd314

Atkins, Stuart, Bd340

Aubéry, Pierre, Bd142-5

Audiat, Pierre, Bd277

Auerbach, Erich, Bd146

Auriant, L., Bb5; Bc12; Bd74, 250-5; Bf3

Austen-Smith, Jane, Bd371

Bachelard, Gaston, Bd100

Baguley, David, Ba3-10; Bb6; Bc13-15; Bd15, 16, 101, 147, 228, 363, 372-4

Bahr, Hermann, Bf4

Bakker, B.H., Ba5-10; Bb7; Bc16, 17; Bg1

Balzer, Hans, Ba11

Bange, Pierre, Bc18

Banville, Théodore de, Bf77

Barbier, Pierre, Be5

Barbusse, Henri, Bb8

Barjon, Louis, Bc19

Baroli, Marc, Bd53

Barrès, Maurice, Bd239; Bh1

Barry, Catherine A., Bc21

Barthes, Roland, Bd256

Baschet, Robert, Bf5

Basdekis, Demetrios, Bc22

Baudson, Pierre, Bc23, 24.

Becker, Colette, Ba12; Bb9; Bc25-30; Bd17; Bf6, 7

Becker, George J., Bf8

Bédé, Jean-Albert, Bb10; Bd1

Bell, David, Bc31

Bellanger, Claude, Bg2

Bellatore, André, Bd375

Bellet, R., Bc32

Bellos, David, Bd148; Bf9

Berg, Walter Bruno, Bd122

Berg, William, Bd149

Bergeron, Régis, Bd321

Bernard, Marc, Bb11, 90

Berteaux, Félix, Bc33

Bertrand-Jennings, Chantal (see also Jennings, Chantal), Bb12; Bc34; Bd244

Bettinson, C.D., Bc35; Bh2

Bevernis, Christa, Bf10

Blanc, Jacques, Bb44

Blankenagel, John C., Bd150

Blasco Ibáñez, Vicente, Bc36

Blaze de Bury, Fernande, Bc37

Block, Haskell M., Bd18

Bloy, Léon, Bd240

Blum, Léon, Bd297

Bonfantini, Mario, Bc38

Bonnefis, Philippe, Bc39-45; Bd54

Bordier, Roger, Bc46

Borie, Jean, Bb13; Bc47; Bd229

Boudry, Robert, Bd298

Boulier, Jean, Bc48

Boulouis, Jean, Bg3
Bourget, Paul, Bc49; Bf11
Bourneuf, Roland, Bc50; Bd75
Boussel, Patrice, Bh3
Boutan, Pierre, Bd19
Bouthoul, Gaston, Bd93
Bouvier, Jean, Bd2, 3
Bouvier-Ajam, Maurice, Bd48
Brachet Pierre, Bd323
Brady, Patrick, Bb14; Bd151, 278, 279
Braescu, Ion, Bc51; Be6
Braibant, Charles, Bc52
Brandes, Georg, Bb15
Braudy, Leo, Bf12
Braun, Sidney D., Bd257
Brombert, Victor, Bd368
Brookner, Anita, Bf13
Brown, Calvin S., Bb16; Bc53, 54; Bd109
Brown, Donald F., Bd110
Bruneau, Alfred, Bb17
Bruneau, Charles, Bc55
Brunetière, Ferdinand, Bc56; Bd299, 305, 324
Brunius, Teddy, Bd280; Bf14
Burns, C.A., Bb23; Bc57-60; Be7
Busquet, Raoul, Bd247
Butler, R., Bf15, 16
Butor, Michel, Bc61; Bd102
Buvik, Per, Bd258

Candille, Marcel, Bd49
Cantoni, Edda, Bc62
Carias, Léon, Bc63
Carol-Bérard, Bd281
Carrère, Jean, Bc64
Carter, A.E., Bc65
Carter, Lawson A., Bb21
Case, Frederick Ivor, Bb22
Cassaing, Jean-Claude, Bc66; Bd300; Be8
Cazaux, Michèle, Bc67
Céard, Henry, Bb23; Bc68
Céline, Louis-Ferdinand, Bc69
Cesbron, Georges, Bd325
Chabaud, Alfred, Bc70
Chaitin, Gilbert, Bd128

Chambron, Jacqueline, Bd20
Chapman, Guy, Bh4
Charensol, Georges, Bf17
Chartreux, Bernard, Bc71
Chemel, Henri, Bg4
Chennevière, Georges, Bc72
Chevrel, Yves, Ba13; Bc73, 74; Bd152, 354
Chiari, Joseph, Bf18
Christie, John, Bc75-7; Bd376
Cirillo, N.R., Bd153
Citron, Pierre, Bc78
Citron, Suzanne, Bd76
Clamens, Pierre A., Bd326
Clark, Roger J.B., Bd259
Clarín [Leopoldo Alas], Bc79; Bd4, 327
Claverie, Michel, Bc80; Bd341
Cocteau, Jean, Bc81
Coeuroy, André, Bc82
Cogny, Pierre, Bb24, 84; Bc83-6; Bd21, 154, 241; Bh5
Cohen, Gaston, Bd5
Colburn, William E., Bc87
Collet, Georges-Paul, Bc88
Conrad, Michael Georg, Bb25
Conroy, Peter V., Jr, Bd260
Cornell, Kenneth, Bc89
Couillard, M., Bc90
Courthion, Pierre, Bf19
Cressot, Marcel, Bd22, 65
Croce, Benedetto, Bc91

Dahlström, C., Bc92
Daix, Pierre, Bf20
Dallenbach, Lucien, Bc93
Dangelzer, Joan-Yvonne, Bc94
D'Annunzio, Gabriele, Bd103
Daudet, Alphonse, Be9
Daudet, Léon, Bc95-9
Daus, Ronald, Ba14
David-Sauvageot, A., Bf21
Davis, Gifford, Bc100
Davoine, Jean-Pierre, Bd23, 155
De Amicis, Edmondo, Bc101; Bg5
Decker, Clarence R., Bc102, 103

Dédéyan, Charles, Bd377

De Faria, Neide, Bb26

Deffoux, Léon, Bb74; Bc104, 105

Delas, Daniel, Bd261; Bg6

De Lattre, Alain, Bb27

Deleuze, Gilles, Bd55

Delhorbe, Cécile, Bh7

De Luca, Giuseppe, Bc106

Dentan, Michel, Bd56

De Sanctis, Francesco, Bc107; Bd24

Descaves, Pierre, Bc108

Descotes, Maurice, Bb28; Bd262

Desprez, Louis, Bb29; Bc109

Desroche, Henri, Bd355-7

Deutsch, Michel, Bb44

De Vogüé, Eugène-Melchior, Bd94

Dezalay, Auguste, Ba15; Bc110-16; Bd77, 129; Bg7; Bh8

Dietrich, Margaret, Be10

Digeon, Claude, Bc117

Donnard, Jean-Hervé, Bd328

Dort, Bernard, Bf22

Doucet, Fernand, Bb30

Drumont, Edouard, Bh9

Dubois, E.T., Bd156

Dubois, Jacques, Bb31; Bc118-21; Bd69

Dubuc, André, Bc122

Duchet, Claude, Bc123; Bd57, 157, 158

Dufay, Pierre, Bd263

Dugan, R., Bd342

Dumesnil, René, Bc124; Bd378

Duncan, Phillip A., Bc125, 126; Bd264, 329; Bg8

Dupuy, Aimé, Bc127-30; Bd50, 70; Bg9

Durand, Gilbert, Bd78

Ebin, Ima N., Bf23

Edwards, Herbert, Bc131, 147

Ehrard, Antoinette, Bc132; Bf24

Ellis, Havelock, Bc133

Engler, Winfried, Bd364

Eoff, Sherman H., Bd159

Ernst, Fritz, Bc134

Esper, Erich, Bc135

Esslin, Martin, Be11

Esteban, Manuel A., Bc136, 137

Euvrard, Michel, Bb35

Fabre, F.-E., Bc138

Faguet, Emile, Bb36; Bd301, 315

Falconer, Graham, Bc139

Farrell, James T., Bf25

Feldman, A. Bronson, Bd58

Féral, Josette, Bd160

Ferragus [Louis Ulbach], Bd343

Field, Trevor, Bd123

Fischer, Ernst, Bc140

Flaubert, Gustave, Bc141

Fol, Monique, Bc299, 300; Bd118

France, Anatole, Bc142, 143; Bd330

Franchi, Danièle, Bd59

Frandon, Ida-Marie, Bb37, 38; Bd161

Franzén, Nils-Olof, Bb39

Fraser, Elizabeth M., Bc144; Bd242

Fréville, Jean, Bb41

Frey, John A., Bb42

Frichet-Rechou, Jacqueline, Be12, 13.

Frierson, William C., Bc145-7

Furst, Lilian R., Bc148; Bd344, 345; Bf26, 27; Bh10

Gahide, Françoise, Bf28

Gaillard, Françoise, Bd25, 162

Gaillard, Jeanne, Bd26

Gauthier, E. Paul, Bc149-51; Bf29

Gauthier, Guy, Bc152

Geffroy, Gustave, Bd163

Genuzio, Joseph, Bb43

Georgin, Robert, Bd164

Gerhardi, Gerhard C., Bd130, 165

Gerland, D., Bd282

Gide, André, Bc153

Gillet, Marcel, Bd166

Gingell, E., Bc154

Girard, Marcel, Ba16, 17; Bb155-9; Bd167, 230

Godenne, Janine, Bd79

Goldenstein, J.-P., Bd141

Goncourt, Edmond and Jules de, Bc160

González de Mendoza, J.M., Bc161

Gosse, Edmund, Bc162; Bd379; Bf30

Got, Olivier, Bc163; Bd131

Gourmont, Remy de, Bc164, 165

Grand-Carteret, John, Bb46

Grant, Elliott M., Bb47, 48; Bc166; Bd60, 80, 132, 168-75, 306, 311, 322

Grant, Richard B., Bb49; Bc167; Bd6, 7, 111

Greaves, A.A., Bc168; Bd66, 112, 113, 358

Gregor, Ian, Bd27

Grobe, Edwin P., Bd28

Gross, David S., Bc169

Gruau, Georges, Bd331

Guedj, Aimé, Bc170; Bd248; Bf31, 32

Guichard, Léon, Bc171; Bd14

Guiches, Gustave, Bd346

Guieu, Jean-Max, Be15

Guillemin, Henri, Bb50, 51; Bh11, 12

Gumbrecht, Hans-Ulrich, Bb52

Günther, Herbert, Bc172

Hambly, Peter, Bd176

Hamilton, George H., Bf33

Hamon, Philippe, Bc173-80; Bd307

Harneit, Rudolf, Bd29

Hart, Heinrich and Julius, Bf34

Hartley, K. H., Bc181

Harvey, Lawrence E., Bd332

Hatzfeld, Helmut A., Bc182; Bf35

Hayman, David, Bd177

Heller, Adolphe B., Bc183

Hemmings, F.W.J., Ba18, 19; Bb53, 54, 193; Bc184-93; Bd114, 115, 178, 231, 380; Be16; Bf36-42; Bg10-12; Bh13

Henderson, John A., Be17

Hérain, François de, Bf43

Heriot, Angus, Be18

Hewitt, Winston R., Bb55

Hoche, Jules, Bc195

Hoefert, S., Bc196

Hoffmann, Frederick J., Bc197

Hofman, Werner, Bb56

Holz, Arno, Bf44

Houston, John Porter, Bc198

Howe, Irving, Bd179

Huret, Jules, Bc199

Huysmans, J.-K., Bb57; Bc200

Ikor, Roger, Bc201, 202

Jackson, Basil, Bd35

Jaeggy, Elena, Bd265

Jagmetti, Antoinette, Bb58

James, Henry, Bc203; Bd266

Jaurès, Jean, Bd302, 359, 360

Jean, Georges, Bc204

Jean, Raymond, Bc205

Jeanne, René, Bc206

Jennings, Chantal (see also Bertrand-Jennings, Chantal), Bc207; Bd267-9, 347

Joachimescu-Graur, Théodosia, Bd8

Johnson, Douglas, Bg14

Joly, Bernard, Bc208; Bd81

Jones, Lawrence William, Bc209

Jones, Malcom B., Bc210

Jouhaux, Léon, Bc211

Jourdain, Francis, Bc212; Bh15

Joyce, William, Bd180

Kahn, Maurice, Bc213

Kamm, Lewis, Bb59

Kanes, Martin, Bb60; Bc214; Bd133, 134, 181, 348; Be19, 20; Bg13, 14

Kantorowicz, Alfred, Bc215, 216

Kayser, Jacques, Bg15; Bh16-19

Kédros, André, Bd30

Keins, Jean-Paul, Bc217

King, Graham, Bb61

Klotz, Volker, Bc218

Knight, Everett, Bc219

Krakowski, Anna, Bb62

Kranowski, Nathan, Bd63

Kuczynski, Jürgen, Bf45

Kuhn, Reinhard, Bd232

Kulczycka-Saloni, Janina, Bc220-2

Laborde, Albert, Bc223-5
Lafargue, Paul, Bd9
Lalo, Charles, Bc226; Bf46
Lambert, Pierre, Bb57
Lanoux, Armand, Bb64; Bc227
Lanson, Gustave, Bc228; Bf47
Lapp, John C., Bb65; Bc229-34; Bd67,
 182, 245, 270; Bf48
Larkin, Maurice, Bc235
Laubriet, Pierre, Bd283
Le Blond, Maurice, Ba20; Bb66, 67; Bc236,
 237
Le Blond-Zola, Denise, Bb68
Le Blond-Zola, Jean-Claude, Bc238, 239
Lecercle, Jean-Louis, Bc240
Ledig, Gerhard, Bd183
Lee, Vernon, Bc241
Leech, Clifford, Bc242
Lefrançois, Philippe, Be21
Legouis, Emile, Bd333
Lejeune, Paule, Bb69
Lejeune, Philippe, Bd184
Lemaitre, Jules, Bc243; Be22
Leonard, Frances McNeely, Bd271
Léonard, Martine, Bd31
Lerner, Michael G., Bc244-8
Leroy, Maxime, Bd32
Lethbridge, Robert, Ba21; Bd82-6
Lethève, Jacques, Bf49
Levin, Harry, Bc249
Lindenberg, Daniel, Bb44; Bd185
Lindsay, Jack, Bc250; Bf50
Livanský, Karel, Bd33
Lloyd, Everett T., Bb70
Lockspeiser, Edward, Bc251
Lombroso, Cesare, Bd61
Loos, Dorothy S., Bc252
López Jiménez, L., Bc253
Loquet, Francis, Bd186
Lorencini, Alvaro, Bb71
Lote, Georges, Bc254; Be23; Bf51
Louis, Paul, Bb72
Lüdeke, H., Bc255
Lukács, Georg, Bc256-8

Lützeler, Paul Michael, Bc259

Macchia, Giovanni, Bc260
Magny, Claude-Edmonde, Bc261
Malinas, Yves, Bd104, 107
Mallarmé, Stéphane, Bb74
Malrieux, Philippe, Bd187
Manceau, Henri, Bd95
Mandin, Louis, Bd349
Manevy, Raymond, Bg16
Mann, Heinrich, Bc262
Mann, Thomas, Bc263, 264
Mansuy, Michel, Bc265
Marcilhacy, Christiane, Bd334
Marel, Henri, Bd188-90
Markiewicz, Henryk, Bf52
Martineau, Henri, Bb75
Martino, Pierre, Bc266; Bf53
Massis, Henri, Bb76
Matoré, Georges, Bd62
Matthews, J.H., Bb77; Bc267-70; Bd63,
 191, 272, 312, 365; Bf54
Maupassant, Guy de, Bb78; Bc271; Bd381
Maurin, Mario, Bc272
Max Stefan, Bb79
McCrossen, Vincent A., Bd243
Melcher, Edith, Be24
Mendès-France, Pierre, Bh20
Menichelli, Gian Carlo, Ba22-4; Bd316
Michot-Dietrick, Hela, Bd34
Milner, George B., Bc274
Minogue, Valerie, Bd116
Miquel, Pierre, Bh21, 22
Mitterand, Henri, Bb80-2; Bc275-84; Bd135,
 136, 192-7, 350, 361; Be25; Bf55;
 Bg17, 18
Monneret, Sophie, Bc285
Montreynaud, Florence, Bc286-8; Bg19
Moody, Joseph N., Bc289, 290
Moore, Charles H., Bd198
Moore, George, Bc291
Moreau, Pierre, Bb83; Bd199
Morgan, O.R., Bc292
Mouchard, Claude, Bf56

Müller, Hans-Joachim, Bf57
Muller-Campbell, Denise E., Bc293
Musumeci, Antonino, Bd117

Naudin-Patriat, Françoise, Bc294
Naumont, Josiane, Bd362
Nelson, Brian, Bd87, 88, 296, 308, 309
Neuschäfer, Hans-Jorg, Bc295; Bd200
Newton, Joy, Bc35, 296-300; Bd35,
    118, 201; Bh2
Nicholas, Brian, Bc301; Bd27
Nicoletti, Gianni, Bd96
Niess, Robert J., Bb85; Bc54, 302-5; Bd36,
    51, 233-6, 284-8, 303, 351; Bf42, 58
Noaro, Jean, Bd273
Nochlin, Linda, Bf59
Noiray, Jacques, Bc306

Ochman, Dániela, Bd37
Oehlert, Richard, Bb86
Olorenshaw, Robert, Bd335
Olrik, Hilde, Ba25; Bd289
Ormerod, Beverley, Bd119
Orr, John, Bd202
Osborne, John, Bc307
Ouellet, Réal, Bc50

Pageard, Robert, Bd336
Pagès, Alain, Bd274; Be26; Bf60
Paisse, Jean-Marie, Bd237
Paraf, Pierre, Bc308; Bd369
Pardo Bazán, Emilia, Bf61
Paris, Renzo, Ba26
Parturier, Maurice, Bb87
Pascal, Roy, Bc309
Pasco, Allan H., Bd120, 203, 290
Patterson, J.G., Bb88
Payot, Roger, Bc310
Péguy, Charles, Bd124
Pelletier, Jacques, Bc311-13
Perruchot, Henri, Bf62
Peter, René, Bc314
Petrey, Sandy, Bc315, 316; Bd38, 39,
    89, 137, 204, 205, 366

Petriconi, Hellmuth, Bd97
Petrovska, Marija, Bd40
Pia, Pascal, Bc317
Picon, Gaëtan, Bc318; Bf63
Pillu, Pierre, Bc319
Place, David, Bd41
Pomilio, Mario, Bc320
Powers, Lyall, Bc321
Pritchett, V.S., Bd42, 291
Proulx, Alfred C., Bb91
Pryme, Eileen E., Be27
Psichari, Henriette, Bb92; Bd206, 207;
    Bh23

Raimond, Michel, Bf64
Raitt, A.W., Bd98
Ramond, F.C., Bb93
Randal, Georges, Bc322
Rannaud, Gérald, Bd208
Raphaël, Paul, Bd138
Rébérioux, Madeleine, Bc323
Rees, Garnet, Bf65
Reizov, B., Bc324; Bf66
Remak, Henry H., Bc325
Reuillard, Gabriel, Bc326
Rewald, John, Bc327-9
Rheims, Maurice, Bf67
Rhodes, S.A., Bd99
Ricatte, Robert, Ba27; Bd139, 382
Richardson, Joanna, Bb96
Richman, Michèle, Bd43
Ripoll, Roger, Bb97; Bc330-2; Bd59, 90,
    121, 209, 249; Bf68; Bg20-22
Robert, Guy, Bb29, 98, 99; Bc333, 334;
    Bf69
Robert, Louis de, Bc335
Roberts, David, Bc336
Robichez, Jacques, Be28
Rod, Edouard, Bc337, 338
Romains, Jules, Bb100
Root, Winthrop H., Bb101
Rosenberg, Rachelle A., Bd210
Ross, Peter, Bd370
Rossat-Mignod, Suzanne, Bc339

Rosselli, Ferdinando, Bc340
Rostand, Jean, Bf70, 71
Roudomino, M., Bc341
Roy, Claude, Bc342; Bd211
Rubenach, Jane, Bc343
Rufener, Helen La Rue, Bb102

Sadoul, Georges, Bc344
Salvan, Albert J., Bb103; Bc345-7; Bd212
Sanders, James B., Bc348; Be29-31
Sarcey, Francisque, Be32
Sarthou, Jacques, Be33
Schächter, Elizabeth Mahler, Bd180
Schalk, Fritz, Bf72
Scherer, Edmond, Bf73
Schmidt, Günter, Bc349
Schober, Rita, Bc350-4; Bd105, 106, 213, 292; Bf74
Schoell, Konrad, Bd383
Schor, Ira N., Bc358
Schor, Naomi, Ba28; Bb104; Bc355-7; Bd44, 71, 140
Schreiber, Till., Bd214
Schulz-Buschaus, Ulrich, Bc359
Scott, J.W., Bd64
Serres, Michel, Bb105
Seznec, Jean, Bf75
Shiff, Richard, Bf76
Sigaux, Gilbert, Bc360
Simon, Pierre-Henri, Bc361
Skrine, Peter N., Bf27
Skwarczynska, Stefania, Bd313
Slater, Judith, Bd72
Smethurst, Colin, Bb106
Souffrin, Eileen, Bf77
Souriau, Etienne, Be34
Speirs, Dorothy, Ba29
Sperco, Willy, Bd317
Stein, Barbara, Bc362
Steinmetz, Jean-Luc, Bc363; Bd293
Steins, Martin, Bd125, 126
Suffel, Jaques, Bc364
Sutton, Geneviève, Bd337
Suwala, Halina, Ba30; Bb81, 107; Bd10, 11; Bf78

Tancock, Leonard W., Bc365; Bg23
Taslitzky, Boris, Bf79
Ten Brink, Jan, Bb108; Bd52, 310
Ternois, René, Bb109, 110; Bc366, 367; Bd215, 238, 275, 294, 318
Tersen, Emile, Bd216
Thalheimer, Siegfried, Bh24
Theis, Raimund, Bd304
Thibaudet, Albert, Bc368-70
Thody, Philip, Bc371
Thomas, Marcel, Bg24; Bh25, 26
Thomson, Clive R., Ba31; Bc372, 373
Tindall, William York, Bc374
Tison-Braun, Micheline, Bc375
Tolstoy, Leo, Bc376
Topazio, Virgil W., Bd217
Toubin, Catherine, Bd107
Toulouse, Edouard, Bb111
Treusch-Dieter, Gerbug, Be35
Trilling, Lionel, Bc377
Triomphe, Jean, Bg25
Trompeo, Pietro Paolo, Bd319
Troy, William, Bd218
Trudgian, Helen, Bf80
Turnell, Martin, Bc378, 379

Ulbach, Louis: see Ferragus

Vallès, Jules, Bc380, 381
Vanhelleputte, Michel, Bc382
Van Tieghem, Bb112
Varloot, Jean, Bf81, 82
Vauzat, Guy, Bd276
Verhaeren, Emile, Bd12
Vernois, Paul, Bd338
Via, Sara, Bd91
Vial, André-Marc, Bb113
Vicaire, Gabriel, Bf83
Vidal, Jean, Bb82
Viens, Jacques, Bb114
Villefosse, Louis de, Bd320
Vincent, Jean-Pierre, Bb44
Vinchot, Jean, Bc383, 384
Vissière, Jean-Louis, Bd45, 219

Wais, K., Bc385

Walcutt, Charles Child, Bc386

Walker, Philip D., Bb115; Bc387-94; Bd46,
173, 220-4

Walter, Gerhard, Bb116

Walter, Rodolphe, Bc395-9; Bd246, 352,
353; Bf84

Weinberg, Henry, Bc400; Bd47, 384, 385;
Bf85; Bg26, 27

Weinstein, Sophie R., Bd68

Weiske, Fritz, Bc401

Weiss, J.-J., Bf86

Wellek, René, Bf87

Wenger, Jared, Bc402, 403

White, Lucien, Bc404-6

Whiting, George W., Be36

Williams, Merryn, Bb117

Wilson, Angus, Bb118

Wilson, Nelly, Bc407; Bh27

Wolfzettel, Friedrich, Ba32; Bc408, 409;
Bd92, 108

Wood, John S., Bh28

Woollen, Geoff, Bd225

Wurmser, André, Bc410, 411; Bd13

Zakarian, Richard H., Bb120; Bd339

Zamparelli, Thomas, Bd295

Zavie, Emile, Bc105

Zéraffa, Michel, Bc412

Zévaès, Alexandre, Bb121, 122; Bc413,
414; Bh29

Zilli, L., Bb123

Zimmermann, Melvin, Bd226

Zucker, A.E., Bc415

INDEX OF NAMES APPEARING (OTHER THAN FORTUITOUSLY)
IN TITLES OR ANNOTATIONS

Alexis, Paul, Bb7; Bc16, 247; Bg1

Antoine, André, Be29, 30

Balzac, Honoré de, Bb72; Bc127, 410;
    Bd1, 133, 255, 283, 285, 328;
    Bf9, 10, 65, 74

Banville, Théodore de, Bf77

Barbusse, Henri, Bc51, 308

Barrès, Maurice, Bc20

Bernard, Claude, Bf80

Blasco Ibáñez, Vicente, Bc137

Boborykin, P.D., Bc287

Boucicaut, M. et Mme., Bd49

Bouhélier, Saint-Georges de, Bc75-7

Bourget, Paul, Bc265

Brahm, Otto, Bc196

Broch, Hermann, Bc259

Busnach, William, Be19, 31

Céard, Henry, Bc57; Bd212

Cézanne, Paul, Bb85; Bc250, 274, 277,
    285, 327, 328, 396

Champfleury, Jules, Bc183

Clarétie, Jules, Bc343

Courbet, Gustave, Bf24, 63

Crane, Stephen, Bc4

D'Antigny, Blanche, Bd263, 276

Daudet, Alphonse, Bc91, 172, 335; Bd178

De Sanctis, Francesco, Bc11, 38

Dickens, Charles, Bd340

Diderot, Denis, Bf31

Doré, Gustave, Bc132

Dreiser, Theodore, Bd18, 345

Dumas [fils], Alexandre, Bc376

Duranty, Edmond, Bb87; Bf3

Eisenstein, Sergei, Bd201

Flaubert, Gustave, Bc5, 122, 150, 214,
    326; Bf39, 41, 65

Fontane, Theodor, Bc18

Fourier, Charles, Bd355-7

France, Anatole, Bc52, 63, 213; Bh24

Gamboa, Federico, Bd284

Garland, Hamelin, Bc4

Gide, André, Bc36

Goncourt, Edmond de, Bc83, 302, 383;
    Bd34, 69

Guesde, Jules, Bb44; Bc413

Guyot, Yves, Bd199

Halévy, Ludovic, Bc229, 233

Hauptmann, Gerhart, Bd150, 198, 323

Hawthorne, Nathaniel, Bd351

Hearn, Lafcadio, Bc345

Hennique, Léon, Bc292

Houssaye, Arsène and Henri, Bd74

Hugo, Victor, Bg21

Huysmans, J.-K., Bc239; Bd241

Ibsen, Henrik, Bc307

James, Henry, Bc321; Bd286

Jonson, Ben, Be36

Lampedusa, Tomasi di, Bd109

Lazare, Bernard, Bh27

Le Blond, Maurice, Bc75

Le Bon, Gustave, Bc268

Leo XIII (Pope), Bc105

Levasseur, Pierre-Emile, Bc28

149

Loti, Pierre, Bd326
Lukács, Georg, Bc311, 358

Mallarmé, Stéphane, Bc363
Malot, Hector, Bf40
Manet, Edouard, Bb85; Bf14, 23, 33, 37, 38
Mann, Heinrich, Bc215, 216, 336, 382
Mann, Thomas, Bc217; Bd18
Maupassant, Guy de, Bc208; Bd373
Michelet, Jules, Bd65
Monet, Claude, Bc398
Moore, George, Bc12, 88, 148; Bd288

Napoleon III, Bb28; Bc128
Norris, Frank, Bb2; Bc4

Pardo Bazán, Emilia, Bc100; Bd110
Pelletan, Eugène, Bg14
Poulot, Denis, Bd21, 32
Proust, Marcel, Bc46

Quinet, Edgar, Bd120

Reinach, Joseph, Bh28
Renan, Ernest, Bf75
Ringuet, Bb114
Rod, Edouard, Bc244-7
Rodin, Auguste, Bc299, 300
Rousseau, Jean-Jacques, Bc361
Roux, Marius, Bc373

Sainte-Beuve, Charles Augustin, Bd348; Bf15
Schopenhauer, Artur, Bc135
Shakespeare, William, Bd333
Solari, Louise, Bc158, 185
Stasyulevitch, M.M., Bf29; Bg18, 19
Steinbeck, John, Bc209
Stendhal, Bc186, 187
Strindberg, August, Bc92

Taine, Hippolyte, Bc248; Bd86; Bf15, 46, 48

Tasso, Torquato, Bd117
Thyébaut, Gabriel, Bc238
Tieck, Ludwig, Be36
Turgenev, Ivan, Bc214, 286, 288

Unamuno, Miguel de, Bc22

Vailland, Roger, Bd364
Valera, Juan, Bc253
Vallès, Jules, Bc32, 62, 138, 319, 414
Verga, Giovanni, Bc181, 366; Bd180
Verne, Jules, Bd354

Wagner, Richard, Bc53, 54, 82, 171, 251

Zola, Mme Emile (Alexandrine), Bc223
Zola, François, Bc26

RESEARCH BIBLIOGRAPHIES & CHECKLISTS

Edited by

A. D. Deyermond, J. R. Little and J. E. Varey

1.	Little, R.	Saint-John Perse: a bibliography for students of his poetry, 1971
		Supplement no. 1, 1976
2.	Sheringham, M.	André Breton: a bibliography, 1972
3.	Sharrer, H. L.	Hispanic Arthurian Material in the Middle Ages: a critical bibliography, 1977
4.	Hoy, P.	Julien Gracq: essai de bibliographie, 1938-1972, 1973
5.	Little, J. P.	Simone Weil: a bibliography, 1973
		Supplement no. 1, 1979
6.	Labriolle, J. de	Claudel and the English-speaking World: a critical bibliography, 1973
7.	Scott, J. W	Madame de Lafayette: a selective critical bibliography, 1974
8.	Wright, B.	Eugène Fromentin: a bibliography, 1973
9.	Wells, M. B.	Du Bellay: a bibliography, 1973
10.	Bradby, D.	Adamov, 1975
11.	Aquila, A. J.	Alonso de Ercilla y Zúñiga: a basic bibliography, 1975
12.	Griffin, N.	Jesuit School Drama: critical literature, 1976
13.	Crosby, J. O.	Guía bibliográfica para el estudio crítico de Quevedo, 1976
14.	Smith, P.	Vicente Blasco Ibáñez: an annotated bibliography, 1976
15.	Duggan, J. J.	A Guide to Studies on the *Chanson de Roland*, 1976
16.	Bishop, M.	Pierre Reverdy: a bibliography, 1976
17.	Kelly, D.	Chrétien de Troyes: an analytic bibliography, 1976
18.	Rees, M. A.	French Authors on Spain, 1800-1850: a checklist, 1977
19.	Snow, J. T.	The Poetry of Alfonso X, el Sabio: a critical bibliography, 1977
20.	Hitchcock, R.	The *Kharjas*: a critical bibliography, 1977
21.	Burgess, G. S.	Marie de France: an analytical bibliography, 1977
22.	Bach, K. F. and G. Price	Romance Linguistics and the Romance Languages: a bibliography of bibliographies, 1977
23.	Eisenberg, D.	Castilian Romances of Chivalry in the Sixteenth Century: a bibliography, 1979
24.	Hare, G.	Alphonse Daudet: a critical bibliography
		I. Primary material, 1978
		II. Secondary material, 1979